Citizenship Made Simple

Citizenship Made Simple
an easy to read guide to the U.S. Citizenship process

by
Barbara Brooks Kimmel and Alan M. Lubiner, Esq.

Published by:
Next Decade, Inc.
(formerly New Decade Inc.)
39 Old Farmstead Road
Chester, New Jersey 07930-2732 USA

Cover design by Lily Secada, Secada Creative, Greenwich, Connecticut

Publisher's Cataloging in Publication
(Prepared by Quality Books Inc.)

Kimmel, Barbara Brooks
  Citizenship made simple: an easy to read guide to the U.S.
citizenship process/ by Barbara Brooks Kimmel & Alan M. Lubiner

p. cm.
Includes index.
Preassigned LCCN: 95-92661
ISBN 0-9626003-3-4

  1. Naturalization-- Popular works.   I. Lubiner, Alan M. II.
Title

KF4710.Z9K56 1996   342. 73'083
                              QBI95-20602

$15.95 Softcover

Table of Contents

ABOUT THE AUTHORS

- Barbara Kimmel spent fifteen years employed in the New York area, as an immigration consultant, with many international companies and several prominent immigration lawyers. During that time she successfully guided thousands of aliens through the immigration process. In 1990 Barbara began writing, publishing and distributing books on immigration and related subjects. Her first book, **Immigration Made Simple,** was published in 1990. This book has received outstanding professional reviews, and has been a Quality Books #1 bestseller. Thousands of copies have been distributed both domestically and internationally. The second edition was published in 1992, and the third edition is to be released in 1996, at the same time as **Citizenship Made Simple**. Barbara is also the President and Publisher at Next Decade, Inc.

  Ms. Kimmel holds a Bachelor of Arts Degree in International Affairs from Lafayette College in Pennsylvania and a Master's Degree in Business Administration from the Bernard M. Baruch Graduate School of Business of the City University of New York.

- Alan Lubiner has been practicing Immigration Law since 1975. From 1975 until 1981, he was employed by the Immigration & Naturalization Service as an Immigration Officer and Attorney. In 1981, Mr. Lubiner opened a private law practice, specializing in Immigration law. He currently maintains offices in Cranford, New Jersey and Edison, New Jersey, and has successfully handled thousands of immigration cases.

  Mr. Lubiner holds a Bachelor of Science Degree in Finance from New York University and a Juris Doctorate degree from Brooklyn Law School. He is a member of the American Immigration Lawyers Association, an affiliated organization of the American Bar Association, and served on its Board of Governors. He is the immediate past Chairman of the New Jersey Chapter of the American Immigration Lawyer's Association. Mr. Lubiner is a member of the Bar of the States of New Jersey, New York and Pennsylvania and is admitted to practice before the Federal Courts in New Jersey, New York and Pennsylvania, as well as the United States Supreme Court.

*With special thanks to all those who continue to recognize
the importance of these valuable reference books*

****

DISCLAIMER

The purpose of this book is to provide interested individuals with a basic understanding of the rules and regulations concerning U.S. Citizenship procedures. It is sold with the understanding that the publisher and authors are not engaged in rendering legal or other professional services in this book, only in sharing information in regard to the subject matter covered. If legal or other expert assistance is required, the services of a competent professional should be sought.

This manual was not written to provide all the information that is available to the authors/and or publisher on the subject of U.S. citizenship, but rather, to compliment, amplify and supplement other texts and available information. While every effort has been made to ensure that this book is as complete and accurate as possible, there may be mistakes, either typographical or in content. Therefore, this text should be used as a general guide only, and not as the ultimate source of U.S. Citizenship information. Furthermore, this book contains information on U.S. Citizenship only up to the printing date. The rules and regulations change frequently.

The authors and Next Decade, Inc. shall not be held liable, nor be responsible to any person or entity with respect to any loss or damage caused, or alleged to be caused, directly or indirectly by the information contained in this book.

**If you do not wish to be bound by the above,
you may return this book to the publisher for a full refund.**

INTRODUCTION

Over the past five years I've been busy writing and updating a book called **Immigration Made Simple, an easy to read guide to the U.S. Immigration Process**. I've been doing this because, from my experience working directly with immigrants and their advisers, I knew that they all shared one common characteristic. They lacked knowledge of the U.S. Immigration process and needed a simple manual that would provide a basic foundation on U.S. immigration regulations. As I had suspected, there certainly was a need for this type of publication. I continue to receive thousands of orders for **Immigration Made Simple** from every state in the U.S., and many foreign countries as well.

Now I have identified another need. More immigrants are applying for U.S. Citizenship then ever before. They need a reference guide that will explain the basic rules and regulations. Now I will try to fill this need with my new book **Citizenship Made Simple**.

Like my book on U.S. Immigration, this book has once again been developed as an easy to use reference for foreign nationals who currently live and work in the United States, and wish to apply for U.S. Citizenship. The book should also be of considerable value to those who teach courses on U.S. Citizenship, English as a Second Language instructors, corporate personnel, educational institutions, business managers, legal support staff, and others who have occasion to work with our U.S. Immigration and Citizenship processes.

The order of the subject matter is intended to be useful. I start by defining some frequently used terms. The sections that follow describe the process of becoming a U.S. Citizen, the requirements, the application procedure, and the test. There is also information on U.S. history, important historical documents, the U.S. government, our holidays, and U.S. Presidents. This is followed by a very important chapter including one hundred questions and answers to be used as a study guide for the U.S. Citizenship Exam. Finally, you will find sample forms, a Directory of Immigration & Naturalization Service Offices and U.S. Passport Agencies.

I would like to thank my co-author, Alan Lubiner, who is an Immigration lawyer, for his expertise and valuable input. Alan's years of experience working for the Immigration & Naturalization Service, as well as in private practice, provide an "insiders" perspective on the U.S. citizenship process.

After you read the chapters that follow, I hope that you will have a better understanding of the process of applying for U.S. Citizenship, and that this book will serve as a helpful reference guide in the future.

Barbara Brooks Kimmel

1 DEFINITIONS

Those applying for U.S. Citizenship will frequently encounter the following terms, and so it is best to know what they mean before reading further.

■ *Alien:* a person who is not a citizen or a national of the U.S. The term refers to all foreign nationals in the U.S., whether they are here temporarily or with permanent resident status. Although the term may seem strange to you, it is frequently used in the immigration field, and therefore in this book.

■ *Beneficiary:* an alien who is the recipient of an application filed on their behalf by another individual or organization.

■ *Citizen:* a person who owes their loyalty to, either through birth or naturalization, the protection of a given country.

■ *Citizenship:* having the status of a citizen, along with its rights, privileges and duties.

■ *Form N-400- Application for Naturalization:* the form that must be completed when applying for U.S. Citizenship. Other documents must accompany this form. See Chapter 5.

■ *Green Card:* a slang term for the identity document or alien registration receipt card issued to permanent resident (immigrant) aliens. The card includes the alien's photograph, fingerprint and signature. At one time the identity card was green, which is how it derived its name.

■ *Immigrant:* an alien who comes to the United States to live permanently.

■ *Immigration and Naturalization Service (INS):* a branch of the United States Department of Justice. The INS is responsible for admitting foreign nationals into the U.S., and processing all immigration and naturalization related applications made by, or on behalf of, foreign nationals. The INS maintains offices throughout the U.S. and in several foreign countries. (See Chapter 14 for a complete list of INS offices in the U.S.)

■ *Naturalization:* a process by which permanent resident aliens can convert their status to U.S. citizenship. Naturalization permits the individual to obtain a U.S. passport and to vote in U.S. elections. Permanent residence and U.S. citizenship are not the same.

■ *Oath of Allegiance:* a formal declaration that must be made when one applies for U.S. Citizenship. See Chapter 4.

■ *Passport:* a document issued by a government that identifies the holder and his citizenship, and permits that individual to travel abroad.

■ *Permanent Residence:* the right to live permanently in the U.S. Individuals are given alien registration cards upon approval of their application for permanent residence and are thereafter called permanent resident aliens. Immigrant is another name for permanent resident alien.

■ *United States:* the geographical territory including the continental U.S., Alaska, Hawaii, Puerto Rico, Guam and the U.S. Virgin Islands.

2 REASONS TO BECOME A US CITIZEN

United States citizenship is desired by people all over the world. They want to become U.S. citizens for many reasons, the most common being:

- **The right to vote**: Only a U.S. citizen can vote in Federal, State and Local elections. This is usually viewed as the most important benefit of U.S. citizenship.

- **Employment**: Certain jobs, including some with the Federal Government, have U.S. citizenship as a requirement for eligibility.

- **Travel with a U.S. passport**: Only a U.S. citizen can travel with a U.S. passport. This right exempts the passport holder from having to apply for visas to enter many countries.

- **Sponsor family members**: U.S. citizens may sponsor their spouse, parents, sons and daughters, and brothers and sisters.

  Note: Legislation is currently pending that, if enacted, would change the rules of sponsorship. Proposed changes include eliminating sponsorship of adult children, as well as brothers and sisters.

- **Freedom from INS scrutiny**: A U.S. citizen cannot be deported.

- **Loyalty and a sense of belonging**: A U.S. citizen can identify with the freedom guaranteed by the United States, a feeling which he or she may or may not have enjoyed elsewhere.

Whatever your reasons, the United States welcomes you.

3 THE FOUR WAYS TO QUALIFY FOR CITIZENSHIP

There are four main ways to qualify to become a citizen of the United States.

1. Through birth in the U.S. :

Almost everyone born in the United States is a U.S. citizen.

2. By birth outside the U.S. :

To parents who are U.S. citizens.

Note: If either or both of your parents or grandparents were, or are, U.S. citizens, consult with an Immigration lawyer. The laws of citizenship are very complicated and have changed many times over the years. You may be a U.S. citizen, and not even know it!

3. After your birth :

By your parents becoming U.S. citizens while you were still a child.

Note: Age restrictions apply, so check with an Immigration professional.

4. Naturalization :

The process of becoming a United States citizen that will be covered in this book.

This page intentionally left blank

Use for notes

4 REQUIREMENTS

In order to be eligible for naturalization you must:

- **Be eighteen years of age or older**

- **Be a lawful permanent resident of the United States**
  (have a green card)

- **Be a permanent resident of the United States for five years**
  (with a green card). If you obtained your green card through marriage
  to a United States citizen, you need only wait three years, instead of five.

- **Have been physically present in the United States for at least
  one half of the required residency period**
  (There are exceptions to this rule)

- **Reside in the State in which you apply for at least three months**

- **Be a person of good moral character**

- **Have the ability to speak, read and write English**
  (there are exceptions to this rule)

- **Have a basic knowledge of the history and government of the
  United States**

(continued)

- ## Have no voluntary Communist affiliation
  (There are exceptions to this rule)

- ## Be willing to take the following Oath of Allegiance to the United States:

Oath of Allegiance

I hereby declare, on oath, that I absolutely and entirely renounce and abjure all allegiance and fidelity to any foreign prince, potentate, state or sovereignty of whom or which I have heretofore been a subject or citizen; that I will support and defend the Constitution and laws of the United States of America against all enemies, foreign and domestic; that I will bear true faith and allegiance to the same; * that I will bear arms on behalf of the United States when required by law; * that I will perform noncombatant service in the Armed Forces of the United States when required by law; that I will perform work of national importance under civilian direction when required by law; and that I take this obligation freely without any mental reservation or purpose of evasion; so help me God.

* In some cases, the INS will allow these clauses to be omitted.

5 HOW TO APPLY

The application for citizenship consists of the following documents:

- **Your cover letter**
- **Form N-400-Application for Naturalization**
- **Fingerprints**
- **Photographs**
- **Copy of front and back of your green card**
- **Filing fee of $95.00**
- **Stamped, self addressed envelope for return of filing receipt**

You can file your Application for Naturalization up to three months in advance of your actual eligibility date.

You must first obtain a Form N-400 and fingerprint chart from the Immigration & Naturalization Service (INS) office that is nearest to where you live. You can request the forms by calling the INS (see list of INS offices in Chapter 14.) There is also a general telephone number to call to request forms: **1-800-870 FORMS**. If you are not sure where to apply, call one of the offices in the State where you live and ask them. Be prepared to hear a recorded message with options you can use when calling from a touch-tone telephone. If you want to speak to an INS representative, you may have to wait for quite a while. You may also visit the INS in person to obtain forms, or you can write and request forms.

Form N-400 must be completed with all the requested information. Do not leave blanks or the INS may send the application back, which will only delay the process.

Your fingerprints can be taken at your local police station, but call ahead to determine the days and times that are available for fingerprinting. **Fingerprints must be completed on the chart supplied by the INS.** In some cities, fingerprints can be taken by private, non-profit organizations such as Catholic Community Services, but you may have to pay a fee. Police stations normally charge a nominal fee, while some will not charge residents of their community. Be sure to complete all information requested on the chart, using black ink or a typewriter.

You will also need two color photographs. The photos should be 2"x2", and you face should be a 3/4 frontal view with your right ear showing. Remove earrings and eyeglasses. (The picture is the same type you needed to obtain when you applied for your green card). A copy of the photograph instructions can be found in Chapter 13. Write your name and alien registration number (green card number starting with "A") on the back of your pictures with a felt tipped pen. Do not staple or bend the pictures.

Your completed cover letter, Form N-400, the fingerprint chart, the two photos, and a copy of the front and back of your green card, together with a check for $95.00, should be sent by certified mail to the INS. (Certified mail is not required, but it is recommended so that you have proof of mailing). Most INS offices will accept a personal check. You may also include a stamped, self-addressed envelope so that the INS office can send you a receipt for your payment. **Make sure to keep a photocopy of your completed application for your records.**

You will receive an appointment in the mail to take your citizenship test. It may take up to eight months to receive the notice.

* Starting in January 1996, applicants for citizenship in the Los Angeles area will begin mailing their applications directly to the INS California Service Center in Laguna Niguel. See Chapter 14 for complete address.

6 The Test

In order to become a United States citizen, you must first prove that you can read, write and speak English, and that you have a basic understanding of the history and government of the United States.

* **Note:** Some people are exempt from the English requirement because of age and long residence in the U.S. If you have been a permanent resident of the United States for at least fifteen years, consult with an Immigration Lawyer to see if you might qualify for an exemption.

You may choose to take the citizenship exam in two ways:

1. As part of a course of study for U.S. citizenship that is offered through an independent organization approved by the INS.

If the applicant passes, he or she will be given a certificate, valid for one year. The INS will accept the certificate in lieu of the written exam, at the time of the naturalization interview.

2. At the INS naturalization interview.

The Immigration Examiner will speak to you in English. He or she will ask you all the questions that are contained on the Form N-400 that you completed. You must show that you understand what the Examiner is asking, and you must answer the questions in English.

You will be asked to write at least one sentence in English, and possibly more if the Examiner has doubts about your ability to write in English. There are no standard sentences. The Examiner will use his or her discretion in determining what to ask, basing their decision on your level of education and background.

You will also be tested on your understanding of the history and government of the United States. The INS Examiner does not expect you to have the knowledge of a college professor, but you are expected to understand our system of government and how it works, how and why our country was founded, and important events in the history of the United States.

The questions you will be asked will usually be taken from the list found in Chapter 12. If you study and learn the questions and answers on that list, you should easily pass the test.

The U.S. Government publishes free study guides, and your Public Library may also have study materials. Ask you librarian for help in finding a book that will aid you in preparing for the U.S. Citizenship test. You can also enroll in a study course given by your local High School or Community College Adult Education Department. Enrollment in such a course is highly recommended for those who do not feel certain about their ability to pass the U.S. Citizenship test.

The application must be approved or denied within four months of the interview. Assuming it is approved, the final swearing-in ceremony will be held the same day, or at a later date, depending on the current procedure at your local INS office. At the time of the swearing-in ceremony, the applicant is required to take the Oath of Allegiance to the United States of America (see complete text in Chapter 4), and sign this oath.

You will then be given a Certificate of Naturalization. With this document, you can obtain a U.S. Passport. See Chapter 15 for addresses of U.S. Passport Offices.

7 A BRIEF HISTORY OF THE UNITED STATES

According to popular history, the United States was discovered in 1492 by Christopher Columbus, an Italian navigator, in service to the King and Queen of Spain. America actually got its name from another Italian navigator named Amerigo Vespucci.

Explorers from England, France and Spain were all trying to claim territory for their homeland. The English claimed the Northeast where the original thirteen colonies were established. The Spanish claimed Florida and surrounding areas, and the French took the land around the Mississippi River.

The first European settlers in the United States were called Pilgrims. They sailed to America on the Mayflower. These English Puritans founded the colony of Plymouth in New England in 1620. Like modern immigrants, they came for a variety of reasons... to escape religious persecution, to claim land for themselves, and to find a better way of life. The American Indians helped the Pilgrims to adjust to their new life in America.

From the late 1600's until the mid 1700's America was the host to several wars fought primarily between the French and the English for control of land. When the French finally lost and ceded all the land east of the Mississippi River to England, the original thirteen colonies were established. The original colonies (the first states) were Connecticut, Delaware, Georgia, Maryland, Massachusetts, New Hampshire, New Jersey, New York, North Carolina, Pennsylvania, Rhode Island, South Carolina, and Virginia.

In the mid 1770's the First Continental Congress met in Philadelphia. It was made up of representatives from all the colonies who were generally upset with their lack of independence from England, their mother country. The following year the Second Continental Congress met and Thomas Jefferson wrote the Declaration of Independence. The colonies essentially declared their freedom from England. When the King and Queen of England learned of this, the Revolutionary War (American Revolution) ensued between England and the colonists, lead by George Washington. On July 4, 1776 the colonies declared their freedom and independence from England and the United States was born, even though the Revolutionary War did not officially end until 1783. One of our famous American Revolutionary leaders was Patrick Henry, who is best known for his slogan "Give me liberty or give me death."

The new Americans wrote the Constitution and appointed their first President, George Washington, in 1789. The United States of America grew and flourished as land was purchased from the French and Spanish.

Land didn't always come easy to the new Americans. The Mexican War was fought against Mexico in the mid-1800's for control of the land now known as Texas. As part of winning the War, the Americans also gained control of land now comprising the States of Arizona, California, Colorado, New Mexico and Nevada. The Americans later fought with Spain in the Spanish American War, winning the U.S. territories of Guam, the U.S. Virgin Islands and the Philippines.

The Civil War, between the Northern and Southern states, was fought from 1861-1865 when Abraham Lincoln was President. The main issue was the abolishment of slavery. The Northern states won the war and slavery was abolished.

The United States also fought in the two World Wars. In World War I, the U.S. sided with England and France against Germany. During World War II, the United States fought against the "Axis Powers" consisting of Germany, Italy and Japan (also Hungary, Romania and Bulgaria). The United States was allied with many countries including Britain, France, the old USSR, Australia and Canada.

Today the United States of America is the strongest nation in the world. We welcome immigrants with the hope that one day each immigrant will choose to become a U.S. citizen.

8 IMPORTANT DOCUMENTS IN OUR NATION'S HISTORY

Some of the more important documents in the history of the United States are:

The Mayflower Compact

On November 21, 1620 forty one of the approximately one hundred passengers who had sailed on the Mayflower from Plymouth England bound for Virginia, signed the Mayflower Compact in Cape Cod Harbor. By signing this document, these Pilgrims, led by William Bradford, had officially selected a place to permanently settle in America.

The Declaration of Independence

This document declared our freedom from England in 1776, and was formally adopted on July 4, 1776. It was written by Thomas Jefferson and signed by the Representatives from the original thirteen colonies, thus beginning our great nation. The basic belief of the Declaration of Independence is "that all men are created equal". The original colonies (the first states) were Connecticut, Delaware, Georgia, Maryland, Massachusetts, New Hampshire, New Jersey, New York, North Carolina, Pennsylvania, Rhode Island, South Carolina, and Virginia.

The entire text of the Declaration of Independence is reproduced at the end of this chapter.

The Articles of Confederation

This was the first Constitution of the United States, adopted in 1781 by the original thirteen states. It remained in effect until 1788 when the present Constitution was ratified.

The Constitution

The Constitution is the "Supreme law of the land". It protects the rights of everyone living in the United States (citizens and non-citizens alike). It was written by delegates of twelve of the original thirteen states in Philadelphia in May 1787. Rhode Island failed to send a representative. George Washington led the session, which lasted until September. It went into effect on the first Wednesday in March, 1789, with New Hampshire casting the ninth vote needed for approval on June 21, 1788. The original Constitution had a Preamble (introduction), and seven parts or Articles.

The Preamble read as follows:

We the people of the United States, in order to form a more perfect Union, establish Justice, insure domestic tranquillity, provide for the common defense, promote the general welfare, and secure the blessings of liberty to ourselves and our posterity, do ordain and establish this Constitution for the United States of America.

The original seven Articles dealt with the following issues:

1. Establishing the Legislative Branch to make the laws
2. Establishing the Executive Branch to enforce the laws
3. Establishing the Judicial Branch to interpret the laws
4. What powers should be given to the States
5. Adding or making changes to the Constitution
6. Handling debts and treaties
7. How many State votes would be necessary to accept the Constitution.

The Constitution can only be changed by an amendment. The first ten amendments to the Constitution were ratified on December 15, 1791 and were named the Bill of Rights. There have been a total of twenty six amendments.

The entire text of the original Constitution is reproduced at the end of this chapter.

Bill of Rights

The first ten amendments to the Constitution became the Bill of Rights. They were:

Article I- Freedom of religion, speech, of the press, and right of petition.

Article II- Right of the people to bear arms not to be infringed.

Article III-Quartering of troops.

Article IV-Persons and houses to be secure from unreasonable searches and seizures.

Article V-Trials for crimes; just compensation for private property taken for public use.

Article VI-Civil rights in trials for crimes enumerated.

Article VII-Civil rights in civil suits.

Article VIII-Excessive bail, fines, and punishments prohibited.

Article IX-Reserved rights of people.

Article X-Powers not delegated, reserved to states and people respectively.

The Monroe Doctrine

This was written by President James Monroe and announced during his message to Congress on December 2, 1823. Basically, it established a policy of opposing interference by other countries, in the affairs of the United States.

The Emancipation Proclamation

This was issued by President Abraham Lincoln on January 1, 1863 and declared freedom for the slaves. It led to the Civil War when the South wanted to secede or separate from the North.

The Gettysburg Address

The Battle of Gettysburg, fought on July 1, 2 and 3, 1863 was one of the most famous of the Civil War. On November 19, 1863, President Lincoln declared the field where the battle was fought as a national cemetery, and delivered a two minute speech, which became known as the Gettysburg Address.

TEXT OF THE DECLARATION OF INDEPENDENCE

In Congress July 4, 1776, The Unanimous Declaration of The Thirteen United States of America

When in the Course of human events, it becomes necessary for one people to dissolve the political bands which have connected them with another, and to assume among the Powers of the earth, the separate and equal station to which the Laws of Nature and of Nature's God entitle them, a decent respect to the opinions of mankind requires that they should declare the causes which impel them to the separation.

We hold these truths to be self-evident, that all men are created equal, that they are endowed by their Creator with certain unalienable Rights, that among these are Life, Liberty, and the pursuit of Happiness. That to secure these rights, Governments are instituted among Men, deriving their just powers from the consent of the governed. That whenever any Form of Government becomes destructive of these ends, it is the Right of the People to alter or to abolish it, and to institute new Government, having its foundation on such principles and organizing its powers in such form, as to them shall seem most likely to effect their Safety and Happiness. Prudence, indeed, will dictate that Governments long established should not be changed for light and transient causes; and accordingly all experience hath shown that mankind are more disposed to suffer, while evils are sufferable, than to right themselves by abolishing the forms to which they are accustomed. But when a long train of abuses and usurpations pursuing invariably the same Object evinces a design to reduce them under absolute Despotism, it is their right, it is their duty, to throw off such Government, and to provide new Guards for their future security. Such has been the patient suffrance of these Colonies; and such is now the necessity which constrains them to alter their former Systems of Government. The history of the present King of Great Britain is a history of repeated injuries and usurpations, all having in direct object the establishment of an absolute Tyranny over these States. To prove this, let Facts be submitted to a candid world.

He has refused his Assent to Laws, the most wholesome and necessary for the public good.

He has forbidden his Governors to pass laws of immediate and pressing importance, unless suspended in their operation till his Assent should be obtained; and when so suspended, has utterly neglected to attend to them.

He has refused to pass other Laws for the accommodation of large districts of people, unless those people would relinquish the right of Representation in the Legislature, a right inestimable to them and formidable to tyrants only.

He has called together legislative bodies at places unusual, uncomfortable, and distant from the depository of their Public Records, for the sole purpose of fatiguing them into compliance with his measures.

He has dissolved Representative Houses repeatedly, for opposing with manly firmness his invasions on the rights of the people.

He has refused for a long time, after such dissolutions, to cause others to be elected; whereby the Legislative Powers, incapable of Annihilation, have returned to the People at large for their exercise; the State remaining in the meantime exposed to all the dangers of invasion from without, and convulsions within.

He has endeavored to prevent the population of these States; for that purpose obstructing the Laws for Naturalization of Foreigners; refusing to pass others to encourage their migration hither, and raising the conditions of new Appropriations of Lands.

He has obstructed the Administration of Justice, by refusing his Assent to Laws for establishing Judiciary Powers.

He has made Judges dependent on his Will alone, for the tenure of their offices, and the amount and payment of their salaries.

He has erected a multitude of New Offices, and sent hither swarms of Officers to harass our people, and eat out their substance.

He has kept among us, in times of peace, Standing Armies without the Consent of our legislatures.

He has affected to render the military independent of and superior to the Civil Power.

He has combined with others to subject us to a jurisdiction foreign to our constitution, and unacknowledged by our laws; giving his Assent to their acts of pretended legislation.

> For quartering large bodies of armed troops among us:
> For protecting them, by a mock Trial, from Punishment for any Murders which they should commit on the Inhabitants of these States:
> For cutting off our Trade with all parts of the world:
> For imposing taxes on us without our Consent:
> For depriving us in many cases, of the benefits of Trial by Jury:
> For transporting us beyond Seas to be tried for pretended offenses:
> For abolishing the free System of English Laws in a neighboring Province, establishing therein an Arbitrary government, and enlarging its Boundaries so as to render it at once an example and fit instrument for introducing the same absolute rule into these Colonies:
> For taking away our Charters, abolishing our most valuable Laws, and altering fundamentally, the Forms of our Governments:
> For suspending our own Legislatures, and declaring themselves invested with Power to legislate for us in all cases whatsoever:

He has abdicated Government here, by declaring us out of his Protection and waging War against us.

He has plundered our seas, ravaged our Coasts, burnt our towns, and destroyed the lives of our people.

He is at this time transporting large armies of foreign mercenaries to compleat the works of death, desolation and tyranny, already begun with circumstances of Cruelty & perfidy scarcely paralleled in the most barbarous ages, and totally unworthy the Head of a civilized nation.

He has constrained our fellow Citizen taken Captive on the high Seas to bear Arms against their Country, to become the executioners of their friends and Brethren, or to fall themselves by their Hands.

He has excited domestic insurrections amongst us, and has endeavored to bring on the inhabitants of our frontiers, the merciless Indian Savages, whose known rule of warfare, is an undistinguished destruction of all ages, sexes and conditions.

In every stage of these Oppressions We have Petitioned for Redress in the most humble terms: Our repeated Petitions have been answered only by repeated injury. A Prince, whose character is thus marked by every act which may define a Tyrant, is unfit to be the ruler of a free people.

Nor have We been wanting in attention to our British brethren. We have warned them from time to time of attempts by their legislature to extend an unwarrantable jurisdiction over us. We have reminded them of the circumstances of our emigration and settlement here. We have appealed to their native justice and magnanimity, and we have conjured them by the ties of our common kindred to disavow these usurpations, which would inevitably interrupt our connection and correspondence. They too have been deaf to the voice of justice and of consanguinity. We must, therefore, acquiesce in the necessity, which denounces our Separation, and hold them, as we hold the rest of mankind, Enemies in War, in Peace Friends.

We, therefore, the Representatives of the United States of America, in General Congress, assembled, appealing to the Supreme Judge of the world for the rectitude of our intentions, do, in the name, and by authority of the good People of these Colonies, solemnly publish and declare, That these United Colonies are, and of Right out to be Free and Independent States; that they are Absolved from all Allegiance to the British Crown, and that all political connection between them and the State of Great Britain, is and ought to be totally dissolved; and that as Free and Independent States, they have full power to levy War, conclude Peace, contract Alliances, establish Commerce, and to do all other Acts and Things which Independent States may of right do. And for the support of this Declaration, with a firm reliance on the Protection of Divine Providence, we mutually pledge to each other our Lives, our Fortunes and our sacred Honor.

TEXT OF THE CONSTITUTION

Preamble

We the People of the United States, in Order to form a more perfect Union, establish Justice, insure domestic Tranquility, provide for the common defence, promote the general Welfare, and secure the Blessings of Liberty to ourselves and our Posterity, do ordain and establish this Constitution for the United States of America.

Article I

Section 1. All legislative Powers herein granted shall be vested in a Congress of the United States, which shall consist of a Senate and House of Representatives.

Section 2. The House of Representatives shall be composed of Members chosen every second Year by the People of the several States, and the Electors in each State shall have the Qualifications requisite for Electors of the most numerous Branch of the State Legislature.

No Person shall be a Representative who shall not have attained to the Age of twenty five Years, and been seven Years a Citizen of the United States, and who shall not, when elected, be an Inhabitant of that State in which he shall be chosen.

Representatives and direct Taxes shall be apportioned among the several States which may be included within this Union, according to their respective Numbers, which shall be determined by adding to the whole Number of free Persons, including those bound to Service for a Term of Years, and excluding Indians not taxed, three fifths of all other Persons. The actual Enumeration shall be made within three Years after the first Meeting of the Congress of the United States, and within every subsequent Term of ten Years, in such Manner as they shall by Law direct. The Number of Representatives shall not exceed one for every thirty Thousand, but each State shall have at Least one Representative; and until such enumeration shall be made, the State of New Hampshire shall be entitled to choose three, Massachusetts eight, Rhode-Island and Providence Plantations one, Connecticut five, New-York six, New Jersey four, Pennsylvania eight, Delaware one, Maryland six, Virginia ten, North Carolina five, South Carolina five, and Georgia three.

When vacancies happen in the Representation from any State, the Executive Authority thereof shall issue Writs of Election to fill such Vacancies.

The House of Representatives shall choose their speaker and other Officers; and shall have the sole Power of Impeachment.

Section 3. The Senate of the United States shall be composed of two Senators from each State, chosen by the Legislature thereof, for six Years; and each Senator shall have one Vote.

Immediately after they shall be assembled in Consequence of the first Election, they shall be divided as equally as may be into three Classes. The Seats of the Senators of the first Class shall be vacated at the Expiration of the second Year, of the second Class at the Expiration of the fourth Year, and of the third Class at the Expiration of the sixth Year, so that one third may be chosen every second Year; and if Vacancies happen by Resignation, or otherwise, during the Recess of the Legislature of any State, the Executive thereof may make temporary Appointments until the next Meeting of the Legislature, which shall then fill such Vacancies.

No Person shall be a Senator who shall not have attained to the Age of thirty Years, and been nine Years a citizen of the United States, and who shall not, when elected, be an Inhabitant of that State for which he shall be chosen.

The Vice President of the United States shall be President of the Senate, but shall have no Vote, unless they be equally divided.

The Senate shall choose their other Officers, and also a President pro tempore, in the Absence of the Vice President, or when he shall exercise the Office of President of the United States.

The Senate shall have the sole Power to try all Impeachments. When sitting for that Purpose, they shall be on Oath or Affirmation. When the President of the United States is tried, the Chief Justice shall preside: And no Person shall be convicted without the Concurrence of two thirds of the Members present.

Judgment in Cases of Impeachment shall not extend further than to removal from Office, and disqualification to hold and enjoy any Office of honor, Trust or Profit under the United States: but the Party convicted shall nevertheless be liable and subject to Indictment, Trial, Judgment and Punishment, according to law.

Section 4. The Times, Places, and Manner of holding Elections for Senators and Representatives, shall be prescribed in each State by the Legislature thereof; but the Congress may at any time by Law make or alter such Regulations, except as to the Places of choosing Senators.

The Congress shall assemble at least once in every Year, and such Meeting shall be on the first Monday in December, unless they shall by Law appoint a different Day.

Section 5. Each House shall be the Judge of the Elections, Returns, and Qualifications of its own Members, and a Majority of each shall constitute a Quorum to do Business; but a smaller Number may adjourn from day to day, and may be authorized to compel the Attendance of absent Members, in such Manner, and under such Penalties as each House may provide.

Each House may determine the Rules of its Proceedings, punish its Members for disorderly Behaviour, and, with the Concurrence of two thirds, expel a Member.

Each House shall keep a journal of its Proceedings, and from time to time publish the same, excepting such Parts as may in their Judgment require Secrecy; and the Yeas and Nays of the Members of either House on any question shall, at the Desire of one fifth of those Present, be entered on the journal.

Neither House, during the Session of Congress, shall, without the Consent of the other, adjourn for more than three days, nor to any other Place than that in which the two Houses shall be sitting.

Section 6. The Senators and Representatives shall receive a Compensation for their Services, to be ascertained by Law, and paid out of the Treasury of the United States. They shall in all Cases, except Treason, Felony and Breach of the Peace, be privileged from Arrest during their Attendance at the Session of their respective Houses, and in going to and returning from the same; and for any Speech or Debate in either House, they shall not be questioned in any other Place.

No Senator or Representative shall, during the Time for which he was elected, be appointed to any civil Office under the Authority of the United States, which shall have been created, or the Emoluments whereof shall have been increased during such time; and no Person holding any Office under the United States, shall be a Member of either House during his Continuance in Office.

Section 7. All Bills for raising Revenue shall originate in the House of Representatives; but the Senate may propose or concur with Amendments as on other Bills.

Every Bill which shall have passed the House of Representatives and the Senate, shall, before it become a Law, be presented to the President of the United States; If he approve he shall sign it, but if not he shall return it, with his Objections to that House in which it shall have originated, who shall enter the Objections at large on their Journal, and proceed to reconsider it. If after such Reconsideration two thirds of that House shall agree to pass the Bill, it shall be sent, together with the Objections, to the other House, by which it shall likewise be reconsidered, and if approved by two thirds of that House, it shall become a Law. But in all such Cases the Votes of both Houses shall be determined by Yeas and Nays, and the Names of the Persons voting for and against the Bill shall be entered on the Journal of each House respectively. If any Bill shall not be returned by the President within ten Days (Sundays excepted) after it shall have been presented to him, the Same shall be a Law, in like Manner as if he had signed it, unless the Congress by their Adjournment prevent its Return, in which Case it shall not be a Law.

Every Order, Resolution, or Vote to which the Concurrence of the Senate and House of Representatives may be necessary (except on a question of Adjournment) shall be presented to the President of the United States; and before the Same shall take Effect, shall be approved by him, or being disapproved by him, shall be repassed by two thirds of the Senate and House of Representatives, according to the Rules and Limitations prescribed in the Case of a Bill.

Section 8. The Congress shall have Power To lay and collect Taxes, Duties, Imposts and Excises, to pay the Debts and provide for the common Defence and general Welfare of the United States; but all Duties, Imposts and Excises shall be uniform throughout the United States;

To borrow Money on the Credit of the United States;

To regulate Commerce with foreign Nations, and among the several States, and with the Indian Tribes;

To establish an uniform Rule of Naturalization, and uniform Laws on the subject of Bankruptcies throughout the United States;

To coin Money, regulate the Value thereof, and of foreign Coin, and fix the Standard of Weights and Measures;

To provide for the Punishment of counterfeiting the securities and current Coin of the United States;

To establish Post Offices and post Roads;

To promote the Progress of Science and useful Arts, by securing for limited Times to Authors and Inventors the exclusive Right to their respective Writings and Discoveries;

To constitute Tribunals inferior to the supreme Court;

To define and punish Piracies and Felonies committed on the high Seas, and Offences against the Law of Nations;

To declare War, grant Letters of Marque and Reprisal, and make Rules concerning Captures on Land and Water;

To raise and support Armies, but no Appropriation of Money to that Use shall be for a longer Term than two Years;

To provide and maintain a Navy;

To make Rules for the Government and Regulation of the land and naval Forces;

To provide for calling forth the Militia to execute the Laws of the Union, suppress Insurrections and repel Invasions;

To provide for organizing, arming, and disciplining, the Militia, and for governing such Part of them as may be employed in the Service of the United States, reserving to the States respectively, the Appointment of the Officers, and the Authority of training the Militia according to the discipline prescribed by Congress;

To exercise exclusive Legislation in all Cases whatsoever, over such District (not exceeding ten Miles square) as may, by Cession of particular States, and the Acceptance of Congress, become the Seat of the Government of the United States, and to exercise like Authority over all Places purchased by the Consent of the Legislature of the State in which the Same shall be for the Erection of Forts, Magazines, Arsenals, dock-Yards, and other needful Buildings;—And

To make all Laws which shall be necessary and proper for carrying into Execution the foregoing Powers, and all other Powers vested by this Constitution in the Government of the United States, or in any Department or Officer thereof.

Section 9. The Migration of Importation of such Persons as any of the States now existing shall think proper to admit, shall not be prohibited by the Congress prior to the Year one thousand eight hundred and eight, but a Tax or duty may be imposed on such Importation, not exceeding ten dollars for each Person.

The Privilege of the Writ of Habeas Corpus shall not be suspended, unless when in Cases of Rebellion or Invasion the public Safety may require it.

No Bill of Attainder or ex post facto Law shall be passed.

No Capitation, or other direct, Tax shall be laid, unless in Proportion to the Census or Enumeration herein before directed to be taken

No Tax or Duty shall be laid on Articles exported from any State.

No preference shall be given by any Regulation of Commerce or Revenue to the Ports of one State over those of another: nor shall Vessels bound to, or from, one State, be obliged to enter, clear, or pay Duties in another.

No money shall be drawn from the Treasury, but in Consequence of Appropriations made by Law; and a regular Statement and Account of the Receipts and Expenditures of all public Money shall be published from time to time.

No Title of Nobility shall be granted by the United States: And no Person holding any Office of Profit or Trust under them, shall, without the Consent of the Congress, accept of any present, Emolument, Office, or Title, of any kind whatever, from any King, Prince, or foreign State.

Section 10. No State shall enter into any Treaty, Alliance, or Confederation; grant Letters of Marque and Reprisal; coin Money; emits Bills of Credit; make any Thing but gold and silver Coin a Tender in Payment of Debts; pass any Bill of Attainder, ex post facto Law, or Law impairing the Obligation of Contracts, or grant any Title of Nobility.

No State shall, without the Consent of the Congress, lay any Imposts or Duties on Imports or Exports, except what may be absolutely necessary for executing it's inspection Laws: and the net Produce of all Duties and Imposts, laid by any State on Imports or Exports, shall be for the Use of the Treasury of the United States; and all such Laws shall be subject to the Revision and Control of the Congress.

No State shall, without the Consent of the Congress, lay any Duty of Tonnage, keep Troops, or Ships of War in time of Peace, enter into any Agreement or Compact with another State, or with a foreign Power, or engage in War, unless actually invaded, or in such imminent Danger as will not admit of delay.

Article II

Section 1. The executive Power shall be vested in a President of the United States of America. He shall hold his Office during the Term of four Years, and, together with the Vice President, chosen for the same term, be elected, as follows

Each State shall appoint, in such Manner as the Legislature thereof may direct, a Number of Electors, equal to the whole Number of Senators and Representatives to which the State may be entitled in the Congress: but no Senator or Representative, or Person holding an Office of Trust or Profit under the United States, shall be appointed an Elector.

The Electors shall meet in their respective States, and vote by Ballot for two Persons, of whom one at least shall not be an Inhabitant of the same State with themselves. And they shall make a List of all the Persons voted for, and of the Number of Votes for each; which List they shall sign and certify, and transmit sealed to the Seat of the Government of the United States, directed to the President of the Senate. The President of the Senate shall, in the Presence of the Senate and House of Representatives, open all the Certificates, and the Votes shall then be counted. The Person having the greatest Number of Votes shall be the President, if such Number be a majority of the whole Number of Electors appointed; and if there be no more than one who have such Majority, and have an equal Number of Votes, then the House of Representatives shall immediately choose by Ballot one of them for

President: and if no Person have a Majority, then from the five highest on the List the said House shall in like Manner choose the President. But in choosing the President, the Votes shall be taken by the states, the Representation from each State having one Vote; A quorum for this Purpose shall consist of a Member or Members from two thirds of the States, and a Majority of all the States shall be necessary to a Choice. In every Case, after the Choice of the President, the Person having the greatest Number of Votes of the Electors shall be the Vice President. But if there should remain two or more who have equal Votes, the Senate shall choose from them by Ballot the Vice President.

The Congress may determine the Time of choosing the Electors, and the Day on which they shall give their Votes; which Day shall be the same throughout the United States.

No Person except a natural born Citizen, or a Citizen of the United States, at the time of the Adoption of this Constitution, shall be eligible to the Office of President; neither shall any Person be eligible to that Office who shall not have attained to the Age of thirty five Years, and been fourteen Years a Resident within the United States.

In Case of the Removal of the President from Office, or of his Death, Resignation, or Inability to discharge the Powers and Duties of the said Office, the Same shall devolve on the Vice President, and the Congress may by Law provide for the Case of Removal, Death, Resignation or Inability, both of the President and Vice President, declaring what Officer shall then act as President, and such Officer shall act accordingly, until the Disability be removed, or a President shall be elected.

The President shall, at stated Times, receive for his Services, a Compensation, which shall neither be increased nor diminished during the Period for which he shall have been elected, and he shall not receive within that Period any other Emolument from the United States, or any of them.

Before he enter on the Execution of his Office, he shall take the following Oath or Affirmation:—"I do solemnly swear (or affirm) that I will faithfully execute the Office of President of the United States, and will to the best of my Ability, preserve, protect and defend the Constitution of the United States."

Section 2. The President shall be Commander in Chief of the Army and Navy of the United States, and of the Militia of the several States, when called into the actual Service of the United States; he may require the Opinion, in writing, of the principal Officer in each of the executive Departments, upon any Subject relating to the Duties of their respective Offices, and he shall have Power to grant Reprieves and Pardons for Offences against the United States, except in Cases of Impeachment.

He shall have Power, by and with the Advice and Consent of the Senate, to make Treaties, provided two thirds of the Senators present concur; and he shall nominate, and by and with the Advice and Consent of the Senate, shall appoint Ambassadors, other public Ministers and Consuls, Judges of the supreme Court, and all other Officers of the United States, whose Appointments are not herein otherwise provided for, and which shall be established by Law: but the Congress may by Law vest the Appointment of such inferior Officers, as they think proper, in the President alone, in the Courts of Law, or in the Heads of Departments.

The President shall have Power to fill up all Vacancies that may happen during the Recess of the Senate, by granting Commissions which shall expire at the End of their next Session.

Section 3. He shall from time to time give to the Congress Information of the State of the Union, and recommend to their Consideration such Measures as he shall judge necessary and expedient; he may, on extraordinary Occasions, convene both Houses, or either of them, and in Case of Disagreement between them, with Respect to the Time of Adjournment, he may adjourn them to such Time as he shall think proper; he shall receive Ambassadors and other public Ministers; he shall take Care that the Laws be faithfully executed, and shall Commission all the Officers of the United States.

Section 4. The President, Vice President, and all civil Officers of the United States, shall be removed from Office on Impeachment for, and Conviction of, Treason, Bribery, or other High Crimes and Misdemeanors.

Article III

Section 1. The judicial Power of the United States, shall be vested in one supreme Court, and in such inferior Courts as the Congress may from time to time ordain and establish. The Judges, both of the supreme and inferior Courts, shall hold their Offices during good Behaviour, and shall, at stated Times, receive for their Services, a Compensation, which shall not be diminished during their Continuance in Office.

Section 2. The judicial Power shall extend to all Cases, in Law and Equity, arising under this Constitution, the Laws of the United States, and Treaties made, or which shall be made, under their Authority;—to all Cases affecting Ambassadors, other public Ministers and Consuls;—to all Cases of admiralty and maritime Jurisdiction;—to Controversies to which the United States shall be a Party;—to Controversies between two or more States; between a State and Citizens of another state;—between Citizens of different States;—between Citizens of the same State claiming Lands under Grants of different States, and between a State, or the Citizens thereof, and foreign States, Citizens or Subjects.

In all Cases affecting Ambassadors, other public Ministers and Consuls, and those in which a State shall be Party, the supreme Court shall have original Jurisdiction. In all the other Cases before mentioned, the supreme Court shall have appellate Jurisdiction, both as to Law and Fact, with such Exceptions, and under such Regulations as the Congress shall make.

The Trial of all Crimes, except in Cases of Impeachment, shall be by Jury; and such Trial shall be held in the State where the said Crimes shall have been committed; but when not committed within any State, the Trial shall be at such Place or Places as the Congress may by Law have directed.

Section 3. Treason against the United States, shall consist only in levying War against them, or in adhering to their Enemies, giving them Aid and Comfort. No Person shall be convicted of Treason unless on the Testimony of two Witnesses to the same overt Act, or on Confession in open Court.

The Congress shall have Power to declare the Punishment of Treason, but no Attainder of Treason shall work Corruption of Blood, or Forfeiture except during the Life of the Person attainted.

Article IV

Section 1. Full Faith and Credit shall be given in each State to the public Acts, Records, and judicial Proceedings of every other State. And the Congress may be general Laws prescribe the Manner in which such Acts, Records and Proceedings shall be proved, and the Effect thereof.

Section 2. The Citizens of each State shall be entitled to all Privileges and Immunities of Citizens in the several States.

A Person charged in any State with Treason, Felony, or other Crime, who shall flee from Justice, and be found in another State, shall on Demand of the executive Authority of the State from which he fled, be delivered up, to be removed to the State having Jurisdiction of the Crime.

No Person held to Service or Labour in one State, under the Laws thereof, escaping into another, shall, in Consequence of any Law or Regulation therein, be discharged from such Service or Labour, but shall be delivered up on Claim of the Party to whom such Service or Labour may be due.

Section 3. New States may be admitted by the Congress into this Union; but no new State shall be formed or erected within the Jurisdiction of any other State; nor any State be formed by the Junction of two or more States, or Parts of States, without the Consent of the Legislatures of the States concerned as well as of the Congress.

The Congress shall have Power to dispose of and make all needful Rules and Regulations respecting the Territory or other Property belonging to the United States; and nothing in this Constitution shall be so construed as to Prejudice any Claims of the United States, or of any particular State.

Section 4. The United States shall guarantee to every State in this Union a Republican Form of Government, and shall protect each of them against Invasion; and on Application of the Legislature, or of the Executive (when the Legislature cannot be convened) against domestic Violence.

Article V

The Congress, whenever two thirds of both Houses shall deem it necessary, shall propose Amendments to this Constitution, or, on the Application of the Legislatures of two thirds of the several States, shall call a Convention for proposing Amendments, which, in either Case, shall be valid to all Intents and Purposes, as Part of this Constitution, when ratified by the Legislatures of three fourths of the several States, or by Conventions in three fourths thereof, as the one or the other Mode of Ratification may be proposed by the Congress; Provided that no Amendment which may be made prior to the Year One Thousand eight hundred and eight shall in any Manner affect the first and fourth Clauses in the Ninth Section of the first Article; and that no State, without its Consent, shall be deprived of its equal Suffrage in the Senate.

Article VI

All Debts contracted and Engagements entered into, before the Adoption of this Constitution, shall be as valid against the United States under this Constitution, as under the Confederation.

This Constitution, and the Laws of the United States which shall be made in Pursuance thereof; and all Treaties made, or which shall be made, under the Authority of the United States, shall be the supreme Law of the Land; and the Judges in every State shall be bound thereby, any Thing in the Constitution or Laws of any State to the Contrary notwithstanding.

The Senators and Representatives before mentioned, and the Members of the several State Legislatures, and all executive and judicial Officers, both of the United States and of the several States, shall be bound by Oath or Affirmation, to support this Constitution; but no religious Test shall ever be required as a Qualification to any Office or public Trust under the United States.

Article VII

The Ratification of the Conventions of nine States, shall be sufficient for the Establishment of this Constitution between the States so ratifying the Same.

Amendments to the Constitution

(The first ten Amendments were ratified Dec. 15, 1791, and form what is known as the Bill of Rights.)

Amendment 1

Congress shall make no law respecting an establishment of religion, or prohibiting the free exercise thereof; or abridging the freedom of speech, or of the press, or the right of the people peaceably to assemble, and to petition the Government for a redress of grievances.

Amendment 2

A well regulated Militia, being necessary to the security of a free State, the right of the people to keep and bear Arms, shall not be infringed.

Amendment 3

No Soldier shall, in time of peace be quartered in any house, without the consent of the Owner, nor in time of war, but in a manner to be prescribed by law.

Amendment 4

The right of the people to be secure in their persons, houses, papers, and effects, against unreasonable searches and seizures, shall not be violated, and no Warrants shall issue, but upon probable cause, supported by Oath or affirmation, and particularly describing the place to be searched, and the persons or things to be seized.

Amendment 5

No person shall be held to answer for a capital, or otherwise infamous crime, unless on a presentment or indictment of a Grand Jury, except in cases arising in the land or naval forces, or in the Militia, when in actual service in time of War or public danger; nor shall any person be subject for the same offence to be twice put in jeopardy of life or limb; nor shall be compelled in any criminal case to be a witness against himself, nor be deprived of life, liberty, or property, without due process of law; nor shall private property be taken for public use, without just compensation.

Amendment 6

In all criminal prosecutions, the accused shall enjoy the right to a speedy and public trial, by an impartial jury of the State and district wherein the crime shall have been committed, which district shall have been previously ascertained by law, and to be informed of the nature and cause of the accusation; to be confronted with the witnesses against him; to have compulsory process for obtaining witnesses in his favor, and to have the Assistance of Counsel for his defence.

Amendment 7

In Suits at common law, where the value in controversy shall exceed twenty dollars, the right of trial by jury shall be preserved, and no fact tried by a jury, shall be otherwise re-examined in any Court of the United States, than according to the rules of the common law.

Amendment 8

Excessive bail shall not be required, nor excessive fines imposed, nor cruel and unusual punishments inflicted.

Amendment 9

The enumeration in the Constitution, of certain rights, shall not be construed to deny or disparage others retained by the people.

Amendment 10

The powers not delegated to the United States by the Constitution, nor prohibited by it to the States, are reserved to the States respectively, or to the people.

9 AN OVERVIEW OF OUR SYSTEM OF GOVERNMENT

The United States is a republic. A republic is a government run by the people through their representatives. These representatives are elected to office by United States citizens, who are allowed to vote for their choice of representatives. Some people call this the "democratic process". President Abraham Lincoln termed this a government "of the people, by the people and for the people". There are two major political parties in the United States, the Republicans and the Democrats. The minimum voting age in the United States is eighteen.

There are four levels of government in the United States.

1. Federal Government

Headquartered in our country's capital, Washington, DC. The Chief Executive of the Federal Government is the President.

2. State Government

Headquartered in the capital of each of the fifty states. The Chief Executive of the State is called the Governor.

3. County Government

Headquartered in the county seat in each county within the State.

4. Local Government

Headquartered in each township, city and municipality in the United States. The Chief Executive of each city or town is usually called the Mayor.

This book will address the structure of the Federal Government. You should have some basic knowledge of your State, County and municipal or local government, as well.

The three branches of the Federal Government are:

- **Legislative**
- **Executive**
- **Judicial**

The **Legislative branch** makes the laws. It is called the Congress and consists of the Senate and the House of Representatives. The Senate has one hundred senators, two from each State. Senators are elected by the people of their State to serve for a six year term. There is no limit on the amount of years they can be re-elected to serve. Senators must be at least thirty years old, and must be citizens of the United States. If a Senator was not born in the U.S., he or she must have resided in the United States for nine years as a U.S. citizen before his or her election. Presiding over the Senate is the Vice President of the United States.

The House of Representatives is the other half of the Legislative branch of government. It is made up of four hundred thirty five representatives, also known as Congressmen, elected by the people of their State. The number of representatives from each State is determined by the State's population. The population is counted every ten years in an official census. A representative serves for a term of two years. There is no limit on the number of years they can be re-elected or serve. Representatives must be at least twenty five years of age and must be citizens of the United States. If a Representative was not born in the U.S., he or she must have resided in the United States for seven years as a U.S. citizen before his or her election. Presiding over the House of Representatives is the Speaker of the House.

The Congress (Legislative Branch) makes the laws. It meets in our Capitol in Washington, DC. Laws start out as bills that are proposed by either the Senate or the House of Representatives. The bill is usually studied and debated by various committees of the Legislature. A law must pass by a majority vote in both the Senate and House of Representatives. It then goes to the President of the United States for signature. It only becomes a law if the President signs. If he refuses to sign, or vetoes the bill, it can still become a law by a two third's majority vote in both the Senate and House of Representatives.

The **Executive Branch** enforces the laws and is made up of the President, the Vice President, fourteen cabinet members (and departments), selected by the President to help him. The President is elected by a group of electors called the Electoral College. As President, he or she also serves as Commander in Chief of the U.S. Military. The President must be at least thirty five years old and must have been born in the United States. He must have resided in the United States for at least fourteen years prior to his election. The President serves for a term of four years and cannot be elected for more than two consecutive terms. Elections are held in November, and the Presidential Inauguration is held the following January. Our first President, "the Father of Our Country", was George Washington. He was also the first Commander in Chief of the U.S. Military. Our current President is William (Bill) Clinton. The President of the United States' official home is the White House in Washington, DC.

The Vice President needs to have the same qualifications as the President since he or she takes over the duties of the President if the President dies, resigns, or is unable to carry out his or her duties. Our current Vice President is Albert Gore.

The Cabinet members are the President's assistants and advisers, and are chosen directly by the President. Their appointment, however, must be approved by the Senate. The Cabinet members hold office until they resign, or until a new President is elected.

The order of Presidential succession is as follows:

1. The Vice President
2. Speaker of the House
3. President pro tempore of the Senate
4. Secretary of State
5. Secretary of the Treasury
6. Continues to 16th- the Secretary of Education.

The **Judicial Branch** interprets the law. At the head of the Judicial Branch is the Supreme Court, the highest court in the United States. The Supreme Court is made up of nine justices or judges. One of them is appointed Chief Justice. Our current Chief Justice is William Rehnquist. They are all appointed by the President and serve for life, or good behavior. The other Federal Courts fall under the jurisdiction of the Supreme Court.

The three branches of government were created and designed to protect our freedom in a system called "checks and balances". This way, the powers of the federal government are divided and balanced so that no one branch can control the people or the other branches. This system is the called the "separation of powers". Our Founding Fathers had experienced the abuses of authority that the English government had inflicted on the colonies, and wanted to prevent the same abuses from occurring in America.

This page intentionally left blank

Use for notes

10 AMERICAN HOLIDAYS AND SYMBOLS

Some of the more important dates celebrated by Americans are:

January 1	New Year's Day
Third Monday in January	Martin Luther King, Jr. Day
February 12	Lincoln's Birthday
February 14	St. Valentine's Day
February 22	Washington's Birthday
Third Monday in February	Presidents' Day
Second Sunday in May	Mother's Day
Fourth Monday in May	Memorial Day
June 14	Flag Day
Third Sunday in June	Father's Day
July 4	Independence Day
First Monday in September	Labor Day
October 12	Columbus Day
October 31	Halloween
The first Tuesday after the first Monday in November	Election Day
November 11	Veterans Day
Fourth Thursday in November	Thanksgiving

New Years Day- A legal holiday in all states. It originated in Roman times, when Janus, a Roman deity with two faces, reflected on the past and looked forward to the future.

Martin Luther King Jr.'s Birthday- Became a legal public holiday in 1986. Honors our late civil rights leader, Martin Luther King.

Lincoln's Birthday- First observed in 1866 when both Houses of Congress gathered to memorialize the assassinated President, Abraham Lincoln. It is a legal holiday in many states.

St. Valentine's Day- A celebration of two martyrs from the third century, who were both named St. Valentine. There are many opinions as to why this day is associated with lovers, but no certain answers.

Washington's Birthday- Begun in 1796 to celebrate the birthday of our first President, George Washington. It is a legal holiday throughout the U.S.

Presidents' Day- Recently, we have begun to jointly acknowledge Presidents of the United States on this day.

Mother's Day- A day to honor all mothers. Originally proposed by Anna Jarvis of Philadelphia in 1907.

Memorial Day- Also known as Decoration Day. A day dedicated to the memory of all those who died in war. Ordered by General John A. Logan, Commander in Chief of the Grand Army of the Republic in 1868. It is a legal holiday in most states.

Flag Day- Commemorates the day the Continental Congress adopted the Stars and Stripes as the U.S. flag on June 14, 1777. It is only a legal holiday in Pennsylvania, but is observed throughout the United States.

Father's Day- A day to honor all fathers. First observed on June 19, 1910.

Independence Day- The day the U.S. adopted the Declaration of Independence (from England) in 1776. It is a legal holiday in all states.

Labor Day- A day set aside to honor all American workers. It was first celebrated in New York in 1882, under the sponsorship of the Central Labor Union. It is a legal holiday in all states.

Columbus Day- Commemorates the discovery of America by Christopher Columbus in 1492. It is a legal holiday in many states.

Halloween- On the Eve of All Saints Day. A day for children in the U.S. to dress up in costumes for masquerades.

Election Day- The date chosen by Act of Congress in 1845 to elect the President of the United States. State elections are usually held on this day, as well. This is a legal holiday in some states.

Veterans Day- Also called Armistice Day until 1954. It commemorates the 1918 signing of the Armistice, ending World War I. It honors all men and women who have served in America's armed forces.

Thanksgiving- Observed nationally since 1941 by Act of Congress, as a day of giving thanks. In America it is believed that Thanksgiving was first celebrated by the American Colonists in 1621, when ordered by Governor Bradford of Plymouth Colony in New England.

The American Flag

The first American flag was reportedly designed and sewn by Betsy Ross in 1776.

Our Flag is red, white and blue, for courage, truth and justice, respectively. Each of the thirteen red and white stripes represents one colony. Each white star represents one of the fifty states in the Union. Hawaii and Alaska are the forty ninth and fiftieth states. We show our loyalty to the flag with the following "Pledge of Allegiance", authored by Francis Bellamy in 1892. The phrase "under God" was not added until 1954.

I pledge allegiance to the flag of the United States of America
And to the Republic for which it stands
One nation under God, indivisible
With liberty and justice for all

The Statue of Liberty

The Statute was given to the United States by France to commemorate the alliance of the two countries in the American Revolution. President Grover Cleveland accepted the statue on October 28, 1886. The Statue of Liberty sits on Liberty Island in New York Harbor. It is a 152 foot high female figure made of steel reinforced copper. The right hand holds a torch and the left carries a table with the inscription: "July IV MDCCLXXVI".

In 1972 President Nixon dedicated the American Museum of Immigration, located at the base of the Statue.

Our National Anthem

The "Star-Spangled Banner" is our national anthem. It was written by Francis Scott Key in 1814, and is sung to the tune "To Anacreon in Heaven". Congress officially made it the National Anthem in 1931. The most popular section of the National Anthem is as follows:

O say, can you see, by the dawn's early light,
What so proudly we hail'd at the twilight's last gleaming?
Whose broad stripes and bright stars, thro' the perilous fight,
O'er the ramparts we watch'd, were so gallantly streaming?
And the rockets' red glare, the bombs bursting in air,
Gave proof thro' the night that our flag was still there.
O say, does that star-spangled banner yet wave
O'er the land of the free and the home of the brave?

Our National Motto

In God We Trust

Our Symbol

The Bald Eagle

Our Currency

The U.S. Dollar

100 Pennies = $1.00
20 Nickels = $1.00
10 Dimes = $1.00
4 Quarters = $1.00

Our national motto "In God We Trust" first appeared on our coins in 1864.

The United Nations

The United Nations came into existence in 1945, and in the Spring of 1951 it established a permanent home in New York City. The organization is comprised of representatives from most countries around the world. The purpose of the United Nations is to promote peace, security and economic development.

11 Presidents of the United States

Bill Clinton is our forty second President. Our Presidents held office in the following order:

1. George Washington
2. John Adams
3. Thomas Jefferson
4. James Madison
5. James Monroe
6. John Quincy Adams
7. Andrew Jackson
8. Martin Van Buren
9. William Harrison
10. John Tyler
11. James K. Polk
12. Zachary Taylor
13. Millard Fillmore
14. Franklin Pierce
15. James Buchanan
16. Abraham Lincoln
17. Andrew Johnson
18. Ulysses S. Grant
19. Rutherford B. Hayes
20. James A. Garfield
21. Chester A. Arthur
22. Grover Cleveland
23. Benjamin Harrison
24. Grover Cleveland
25. William McKinley
26. Theodore Roosevelt
27. William H. Taft
28. Woodrow Wilson
29. Warren G. Harding
30. Calvin Coolidge
31. Herbert Hoover
32. Franklin D. Roosevelt
33. Harry S. Truman

34. Dwight D. Eisenhower
35. John F. Kennedy
36. Lyndon B. Johnson
37. Richard M. Nixon
38. Gerald R. Ford
39. James Earl Carter
40. Ronald Reagan
41. George Bush
42. William (Bill) Clinton

12 SAMPLE QUESTIONS AND ANSWERS

QUESTIONS

1. What are the colors of our flag? _____

2. How many stars are in our flag? _____

3. What color are the stars on our flag? _____

4. What do the stars on the flag mean? _____

5. How many stripes are on the flag? _____

6. What color are the stripes? _____

7. What do the stripes on the flag mean? _____

8. How many states are there in the Union? _____

9. What is the 4th of July? _____

10 What is the date of Independence Day? _____

11. From what country did the colonies declare Independence? _____

12. What country did we fight during the Revolutionary War? _____

13. Who was the first President of the United States? _____

14. Who is the President of the United States today? _____

15. Who is the Vice President of the United States? _____

16. Who elects the President of the United States? _____

17. Who becomes President of the United States
if the President should die? _____

18. For how long do we elect the President? _____

19. What is the Constitution? _____

20. Can the Constitution be changed? _____

21. What do we call a change to the Constitution? _____

22. How many changes or amendments
    are there to the Constitution? _____

23. How many branches are there in our government? _____

24. What are the three branches of our government? _____

25. What is the legislative branch of our government? _____

26. Who makes the laws in the United States? _____

27. What is Congress? _____

28. What are the duties of Congress? _____

29. Who elects Congress? _____

30. How many senators are there in Congress? _____

31. Can you name the two
    senators from your state? _____

32. For how long do we elect each senator? _____

33. How many representatives are there in Congress? _____

34. For how long do we elect the representatives? _____

35. What is the executive branch of our government? _____

36. What is the judicial branch of our government? _____

37. What are the duties of the Supreme Court? _____

38. What is the "Supreme law of the United States"? _____

39. What is the Bill of Rights? _____

40. What is the capital of your state? _____

41. Who is the current Governor of your state? _____

42. Who becomes President of the United States if the President and the Vice President should die? _____

43. Who is the Chief Justice of the Supreme Court? _____

44. Can you name the thirteen original states? _____

45. Who said, "Give me liberty or give me death"? _____

46. Which major countries were our enemies during World War II? _____

47. What are the 49th and 50th states of the Union? _____

48. How many terms can a President serve? _____

49. Who was Martin Luther King, Jr.? _____

50. Who is the head of your local government? _____

51. According to the Constitution, a person must meet certain requirements in order to be eligible to become President. Name one of these requirements? _____

52. Why are there one hundred Senators in the Senate? _____

53. Who selects the Supreme Court Justice? _____

54. How many Supreme Court Justices are there? _____

55. Why did the Pilgrims come to America? _____

56. What is the head executive of a state government called? _____

57. What is the head executive of a city government called? _____

58. What holiday was celebrated for the first time by the American Colonists? _____

59. Who was the main writer of the Declaration of Independence? _____

60. When was the Declaration of Independence adopted? _____

61. What is the basic belief of the Declaration of Independence? _____

62. What is the national anthem of the United States? _____

63. Who wrote the Star Spangled Banner? _____

64. Where does freedom of speech come from? _____

65. What is the minimum voting age in the United States? _____

66. Who signs bills into law? _____

67. What is the highest court in the United States? _____

68. Who was President during the Civil War? _____

69. What did the Emancipation Proclamation do? _____

70. What special group advises the President? _____

71. Which President is called the "Father of our Country" ? _____

72. What Immigration and Naturalization Service form is used to apply to become a naturalized citizen? _____

73. Who helped the pilgrims in America? _____

74. What is the name of the ship that brought the Pilgrims to America? _____

75. What were the thirteen original states of the U.S. called? _____

76. Name three rights or freedoms guaranteed by the Bill or Rights? _____

77. Who has the power to declare war? _____

78. What kind of government does the United States have? _____

79. Which President freed the slaves? _____

80. In what year was the Constitution written? _____

81. What are the first 10 amendments to the Constitution called? _____

82. What is one main purpose of the United Nations? _____

83. Where does Congress meet? _____

84. Whose rights are guaranteed by the Constitution and the Bill of Rights? _____

85. What is the introduction to the Constitution called? _____

86. Name one benefit of being a citizen of the United States? _____

87. What is the most important right granted
    to U.S. Citizens? _____

88. What is the United States Capitol? _____

89. What is the White House? _____

90. Where is the White House located? _____

91. What is the name of the President's official home? _____

92. Name one right guaranteed by
    the first amendment? _____

93. Who is the Commander in Chief of the U.S. Military? _____

94. Which president was the first Commander in
    Chief of the U.S. Military? _____

95. In what month do we vote for the President? _____

96. In what month is the new President inaugurated? _____

97. How many times may a Congressman be re-elected? _____

98. How many times may a Senator be re-elected? _____

99. What are the two major political parties
    in the U.S. today? _____

100. How many states are there in the United States? _____

ANSWERS

1. Red, White and Blue

2. Fifty (50)

3. White

4. One for each state in the union

5. Thirteen (13)

6. Red and White

7. They represent the original thirteen states

8. Fifty (50)

9. Independence Day

10. July 4th

11. England

12. England

13. George Washington

14. William Clinton

15. Albert Gore

16. The Electoral College

17. Vice President

18. Four years

19. The Supreme law of the land

20. Yes

21. Amendments

22. Twenty six (26)

23. Three (3)

24. Legislative, Executive and Judicial

25. Congress

26. Congress

27. The Senate and the House of Representatives

28. To make laws

29. The people

30. One hundred (100)

31. Lautenberg, Bradley (New Jersey)

32. Six years

33. Four hundred thirty five (435)

34. Two years

35. The President, Cabinet, and departments under the cabinet members

36. The Supreme Court

37. To interpret laws

38. The Constitution

39. The first ten amendments of the Constitution

40. Trenton (New Jersey)

41. Whitman (New Jersey)

42. Speaker of the House of Representatives

43. William Rehnquist

44. Connecticut, New Hampshire, New York, New Jersey, Massachusetts, Pennsylvania, Delaware, Virginia, North Carolina, South Carolina, Georgia, Rhode Island, and Maryland

45. Patrick Henry

46. Germany, Italy, and Japan

47. Hawaii and Alaska

48. Two

49. A civil rights leader

50. (insert local information)

51. Must be a natural born citizen of the United States: Must be at least thirty five years old by the time he/she will serve; must have lived in the United States for at least fourteen years.

52. Two from each state.

53. The President

54. Nine (9)

55. For religious freedom

56. Governor

57. Mayor

58. Thanksgiving

59. Thomas Jefferson

60. July 4, 1776

61. That all men are created equal

62. The Star Spangled Banner

63. Francis Scott Key

64. The Bill of Rights

65. Eighteen (18)

66. The President

67. The Supreme Court

68. Abraham Lincoln

69. Freed many slaves

70. The Cabinet

71. George Washington

72. Form N-400, "Application for Naturalization"

73. The American Indians (Native Americans)

74. The Mayflower

75. The Colonies

76.

 • The right of freedom of speech, press, religion, peaceable assembly and requesting change of government.

 • The right to bear arms (the right to have weapons or own a gun, though subject to certain regulations).

 • The government may not quarter, or house, soldiers in the people's homes during peacetime without the people's consent.

 • The government may not search or take a person's property without a warrant.

 • A person may not be tried twice for the same crime and does not have to testify against him/herself.

 • A person charged with a crime still has some rights, such as the right to a trial and to have a lawyer.

 • The right to trial by jury in most cases.

 • Protects people against excessive or unreasonable fines or cruel and unusual punishment.

 • The people have rights other than those mentioned in the Constitution.

 • Any power not given to the Federal Government by the Constitution is a power of either the State or the people.

77. The Congress

78. Republic

79. Abraham Lincoln

80. 1787

57

81. The Bill of Rights

82. For countries to discuss and resolve world conflicts

83. In the Capitol in Washington, DC

84. Everyone (citizens and non-citizens living in the U.S.)

85. The Preamble to the Constitution

86. Obtain Federal Government jobs; travel with a U.S. passport; petition for close relatives to come to the U.S. to live.

87. The right to vote

88. The place where Congress meets

89. The President's official home

90. Washington, DC (1600 Pennsylvania Avenue, NW)

91. The White House

92. Freedom of: speech, press, religion, right of petition

93. The President

94. George Washington

95. November

96. January

97. There is no limit

98. There is no limit

99. Democratic and Republican

100. Fifty (50)

13 FORMS

The following pages contain samples of the documents you will need to file your Application for Citizenship including a cover letter, Form N-400 with instructions, photo specifications and a sample of the fingerprint chart.

Here is a Sample Cover Letter:

Immigration and Naturalization Service
Federal Building
970 Broad Street
Newark, New Jersey 07102

Re: N-400 Application for Citizenship
My Name: John Jones
My Alien Registration Number: A12 345 678

Dear Immigration Officer:

I am enclosing the following documents to support my Application for Citizenship:

      1. Form N-400
      2. Copy of my alien registration card (both sides)
      3. Fingerprints
      4. Photographs
      5. Filing fee of $95.00-check #123456
      6. Stamped, self addressed envelope for return of filing receipt

Sincerely,

Your Signature

INSTRUCTIONS

Purpose of This Form.

This form is for use to apply to become a naturalized citizen of the United States.

Who May File.

You may apply for naturalization if:

- you have been a lawful permanent resident for five years;
- you have been a lawful permanent resident for three years, have been married to a United States citizen for those three years, and continue to be married to that U.S. citizen;
- you are the lawful permanent resident child of United States citizen parents; or
- you have qualifying military service.

Children under 18 may automatically become citizens when their parents naturalize. You may inquire at your local Service office for further information. If you do not meet the qualifications listed above but believe that you are eligible for naturalization, you may inquire at your local Service office for additional information.

General Instructions.

Please answer all questions by typing or clearly printing in black ink. Indicate that an item is not applicable with "N/A". If an answer is "none," write "none". If you need extra space to answer any item, attach a sheet of paper with your name and your alien registration number (A#), if any, and indicate the number of the item.

Every application must be properly signed and filed with the correct fee. If you are under 18 years of age, your parent or guardian must sign the application.

If you wish to be called for your examination at the same time as another person who is also applying for naturalization, make your request on a separate cover sheet. Be sure to give the name and alien registration number of that person.

Initial Evidence Requirements.

You must file your application with the following evidence:

A copy of your alien registration card.

Photographs. You must submit two color photographs of yourself taken within 30 days of this application. These photos must be glossy, unretouched and unmounted, and have a white background. Dimension of the face should be about 1 inch from chin to top of hair. Face should be 3/4 frontal view of right side with right ear visible. Using pencil or felt pen, lightly print name and A#, if any, on the back of each photo. This requirement may be waived by the Service if you can establish that you are confined because of age or physical infirmity.

Fingerprints. If you are between the ages of 14 and 75, you must sumit your fingerprints on Form FD-258. Fill out the form and write your Alien Registration Number in the space marked "Your No. OCA" or "Miscellaneous No. MNU". Take the chart and these instructions to a police station, sheriff's office or an office of this Service, or other reputable person or organization for fingerprinting. (You should contact the police or sheriff's office before going there since some of these offices do not take fingerprints for other government agencies.) You must sign the chart in the presence of the person taking your fingerprints and have that person sign his/her name, title, and the date in the space provided. Do not bend, fold, or crease the fingerprint chart.

U.S. Military Service. If you have ever served in the Armed Forces of the United States at any time, you must submit a completed Form G-325B. If your application is based on your military service you must also submit Form N-426, "Request for Certification of Military or Naval Service."

Application for Child. If this application is for a permanent resident child of U.S. citizen parents, you must also submit copies of the child's birth certificate, the parents' marriage certificate, and evidence of the parents' U.S. citizenship. If the parents are divorced, you must also submit the divorce decree and evidence that the citizen parent has legal custody of the child.

Where to File.

File this application at the local Service office having jurisdiction over your place of residence.

Fee.

The fee for this application is $95.00. The fee must be submitted in the exact amount. It cannot be refunded. DO NOT MAIL CASH.

All checks and money orders must be drawn on a bank or other institution located in the United States and must be payable in United States currency. The check or money order should be made payable to the Immigration and Naturalization Service, except that:

- If you live in Guam, and are filing this application in Guam, make your check or money order payable to the "Treasurer, Guam."
- If you live in the Virgin Islands, and are filing this application in the Virgin Islands, make your check or money order payable to the "Commissioner of Finance of the Virgin Islands."

Checks are accepted subject to collection. An uncollected check will render the application and any document issued invalid. A charge of $5.00 will be imposed if a check in payment of a fee is not honored by the bank on which it is drawn.

Form N-400 (Rev. 07/17/91) N

Processing Information.

Rejection. Any application that is not signed or is not accompanied by the proper fee will be rejected with a notice that the application is deficient. You may correct the deficiency and resubmit the application. However, an application is not considered properly filed until it is accepted by the Service.

Requests for more information. We may request more information or evidence. We may also request that you submit the originals of any copy. We will return these originals when they are no longer required.

Interview. After you file your application, you will be notified to appear at a Service office to be examined under oath or affirmation. This interview may not be waived. If you are an adult, you must show that you have a knowledge and understanding of the history, principles, and form of government of the United States. There is no exemption from this requirement.

You will also be examined on your ability to read, write, and speak English. If on the date of your examination you are more than 50 years of age and have been a lawful permanent resident for 20 years or more, or you are 55 years of age and have been a lawful permanent resident for at least 15 years, you will be exempt from the English language requirements of the law. If you are exempt, you may take the examination in any language you wish.

Oath of Allegiance. If your application is approved, you will be required to take the following oath of allegiance to the United States in order to become a citizen:

"I hereby declare, on oath, that I absolutely and entirely renounce and abjure all allegiance and fidelity to any foreign prince, potentate, state or sovereignty, of whom or which I have heretofore been a subject or citizen; that I will support and defend the Constitution and laws of the United States of America against all enemies, foreign and domestic; that I will bear true faith and allegiance to the same; that I will bear arms on behalf of the United States when required by the law; that I will perform noncombatant service in the armed forces of the United States when required by the law; that I will perform work of national importance under civilian direction when required by the law; and that I take this obligation freely without any mental reservation or purpose of evasion; so help me God."

If you cannot promise to bear arms or perform noncombatant service because of religious training and belief, you may omit those statements when taking the oath. "Religious training and belief" means a person's belief in relation to a Supreme Being involving duties superior to those arising from any human relation, but does not include essentially political, sociological, or philosophical views or merely a personal moral code.

Oath ceremony. You may choose to have the oath of allegiance administered in a ceremony conducted by the Service or request to be scheduled for an oath ceremony in a court that has jurisdiction over the applicant's place of residence. At the time of your examination you will be asked to elect either form of ceremony. You will become a citizen on the date of the oath ceremony and the Attorney General will issue a Certificate of Naturalization as evidence of United States citizenship.

If you wish to change your name as part of the naturalization process, you will have to take the oath in court.

Penalties.

If you knowingly and willfully falsify or conceal a material fact or submit a false document with this request, we will deny the benefit you are filing for, and may deny any other immigration benefit. In addition, you will face severe penalties provided by law, and may be subject to criminal prosecution.

Privacy Act Notice.

We ask for the information on this form, and associated evidence, to determine if you have established eligibility for the immigration benefit you are filing for. Our legal right to ask for this information is in 8 USC 1439, 1440, 1443, 1445, 1446, and 1452. We may provide this information to other government agencies. Failure to provide this information, and any requested evidence, may delay a final decision or result in denial of your request.

Paperwork Reduction Act Notice.

We try to create forms and instructions that are accurate, can be easily understood, and which impose the least possible burden on you to provide us with information. Often this is difficult because some immigration laws are very complex. Accordingly, the reporting burden for this collection of information is computed as follows: (1) learning about the law and form, 20 minutes; (2) completing the form, 25 minutes; and (3) assembling and filing the application (includes statutory required interview and travel time, after filing of application), 3 hours and 35 minutes, for an estimated average of 4 hours and 20 minutes per response. If you have comments regarding the accuracy of this estimate, or suggestions for making this form simpler, you can write to both the Immigration and Naturalization Service, 425 I Street, N.W., Room 5304, Washington, D.C. 20536; and the Office of Management and Budget, Paperwork Reduction Project, OMB No. 1115-0009, Washington, D.C. 20503.

START HERE - Please Type or Print

Part 1. Information about you.

Family Name	Given Name	Middle Initial

U.S. Mailing Address - Care of

Street Number and Name	Apt. #

City	County

State	ZIP Code

Date of Birth (month/day/year)	Country of Birth

Social Security #	A #

Part 2. Basis for Eligibility (check one).

a. ☐ I have been a permanent resident for at least five (5) years.

b. ☐ I have been a permanent resident for at least three (3) years and have been married to a United States Citizen for those three years.

c. ☐ I am a permanent resident child of United States citizen parent(s)

d. ☐ I am applying on the basis of qualifying military service in the Armed Forces of the U.S. and have attached completed Forms N-426 and G-325B

e. ☐ Other. (Please specify section of law) _____

Part 3. Additional information about you.

Date you became a permanent resident (month/day/year)	Port admitted with an immigrant visa or INS office where granted adjustment of status.

Citizenship

Name on alien registration card (if different than in Part 1)

Other names used since you became a permanent resident (including maiden name)

Sex ☐ Male ☐ Female	Height	Marital Status: ☐ Single ☐ Married ☐ Divorced ☐ Widowed

Can you speak, read and write English ?   ☐No ☐Yes.

Absences from the U.S.:

Have you been absent from the U.S. since becoming a permanent resident?   ☐ No ☐Yes.

If you answered **"Yes"**, complete the following. Begin with your most recent absence. If you need more room to explain the reason for an absence or to list more trips, continue on separate paper.

Date left U.S.	Date returned	Did absence last 6 months or more?	Destination	Reason for trip
		☐ Yes ☐ No		
		☐ Yes ☐ No		
		☐ Yes ☐ No		
		☐ Yes ☐ No		
		☐ Yes ☐ No		
		☐ Yes ☐ No		

FOR INS USE ONLY

Returned	Receipt

Resubmitted

Reloc Sent

Reloc Rec'd

☐ Applicant Interviewed

At interview
☐ request naturalization ceremony at court

Remarks

Action

To Be Completed by *Attorney or Representative*, if any
☐ Fill in box if G-28 is attached to represent the applicant

VOLAG#

ATTY State License #

Part 4. Information about your residences and employment.

A. List your addresses during the last five (5) years or since you became a permanent resident, whichever is less. Begin with your current address. If you need more space, continue on separate paper:

Street Number and Name, City, State, Country, and Zip Code	Dates (month/day/year)	
	From	To

B. List your employers during the last five (5) years. List your present or most recent employer first. If none, write "None". If you need more space, continue on separate paper.

Employer's Name	Employer's Address Street Name and Number - City, State and ZIP Code	Dates Employed (month/day/year) From	To	Occupation/position

Part 5. Information about your marital history.

A. Total number of times you have been married _____ . If you are now married, complete the following regarding your husband or wife.

Family name	Given name	Middle initial

Address

Date of birth (month/day/year)	Country of birth	Citizenship
Social Security#	A# (if applicable)	Immigration status (If not a U.S. citizen)

Naturalization (If applicable)
(month/day/year)   Place   (City, State)

If you have ever previously been married or if your current spouse has been previously married, please provide the following on separate paper: Name of prior spouse, date of marriage, date marriage ended, how marriage ended and immigration status of prior spouse.

Part 6. Information about your children.

B. Total Number of Children _____ . Complete the following information for each of your children. If the child lives with you, state "with me" in the address column; otherwise give city/state/country of child's current residence. If deceased, write "deceased" in the address column. If you need more space, continue on separate paper.

Full name of child	Date of birth	Country of birth	Citizenship	A - Number	Address

Form N-400 (Rev 07/17/91)N   *Continued on next page*   63

Part 7. Additional eligibility factors.

Please answer each of the following questions. If your answer is "Yes", explain on a separate paper.

1. Are you now, or have you ever been a member of, or in any way connected or associated with the Communist Party, or ever knowingly aided or supported the Communist Party directly, or indirectly through another organization, group or person, or ever advocated, taught, believed in, or knowingly supported or furthered the interests of communism? ☐ Yes ☐ No

2. During the period March 23, 1933 to May 8, 1945, did you serve in, or were you in any way affiliated with, either directly or indirectly, any military unit, paramilitary unit, police unit, self-defense unit, vigilante unit, citizen unit of the Nazi party or SS, government agency or office, extermination camp, concentration camp, prisoner of war camp, prison, labor camp, detention camp or transit camp, under the control or affiliated with:

    a. The Nazi Government of Germany? ☐ Yes ☐ No

    b. Any government in any area occupied by, allied with, or established with the assistance or cooperation of, the Nazi Government of Germany? ☐ Yes ☐ No

3. Have you at any time, anywhere, ever ordered, incited, assisted, or otherwise participated in the persecution of any person because of race, religion, national origin, or political opinion? ☐ Yes ☐ No

4. Have you ever left the United States to avoid being drafted into the U.S. Armed Forces? ☐ Yes ☐ No

5. Have you ever failed to comply with Selective Service laws? ☐ Yes ☐ No

If you have registered under the Selective Service laws, complete the following information:

    Selective Service Number: _____ Date Registered: _____

If you registered before 1978, also provide the following:

    Local Board Number: _____ Classification: _____

6. Did you ever apply for exemption from military service because of alienage, conscientious objections or other reasons? ☐ Yes ☐ No

7. Have you ever deserted from the military, air or naval forces of the United States? ☐ Yes ☐ No

8. Since becoming a permanent resident, have you ever failed to file a federal income tax return? ☐ Yes ☐ No

9. Since becoming a permanent resident, have you filed a federal income tax return as a nonresident or failed to file a federal return because you considered yourself to be a nonresident? ☐ Yes ☐ No

10. Are deportation proceedings pending against you, or have you ever been deported, or ordered deported, or have you ever applied for suspension of deportation? ☐ Yes ☐ No

11. Have you ever claimed in writing, or in any way, to be a United States citizen? ☐ Yes ☐ No

12. Have you ever:

    a. been a habitual drunkard? ☐ Yes ☐ No

    b. advocated or practiced polygamy? ☐ Yes ☐ No

    c. been a prostitute or procured anyone for prostitution? ☐ Yes ☐ No

    d. knowingly and for gain helped any alien to enter the U.S. illegally? ☐ Yes ☐ No

    e. been an illicit trafficker in narcotic drugs or marijuana? ☐ Yes ☐ No

    f. received income from illegal gambling? ☐ Yes ☐ No

    g. given false testimony for the purpose of obtaining any immigration benefit? ☐ Yes ☐ No

13. Have you ever been declared legally incompetent or have you ever been confined as a patient in a mental institution? ☐ Yes ☐ No

14. Were you born with, or have you acquired in same way, any title or order of nobility in any foreign State? ☐ Yes ☐ No

15. Have you ever:

    a. knowingly committed any crime for which you have not been arrested? ☐ Yes ☐ No

    b. been arrested, cited, charged, indicted, convicted, fined or imprisoned for breaking or violating any law or ordinance excluding traffic regulations? ☐ Yes ☐ No

(If you answer yes to 15, in your explanation give the following information for each incident or occurrence the **city**, **state**, and **country**, where the offense took place, the **date** and **nature** of the offense, and the **outcome** or **disposition** of the case).

Part 8. Allegiance to the U.S.

If your answer to any of the following questions is "NO", attach a full explanation:

1. Do you believe in the Constitution and form of government of the U.S.? ☐ Yes ☐ No
2. Are you willing to take the full Oath of Allegiance to the U.S.? (see instructions) ☐ Yes ☐ No
3. If the law requires it, are you willing to bear arms on behalf of the U.S.? ☐ Yes ☐ No
4. If the law requires it, are you willing to perform noncombatant services in the Armed Forces of the U.S.? ☐ Yes ☐ No
5. If the law requires it, are you willing to perform work of national importance under civilian direction? ☐ Yes ☐ No

Continued on back

Form N-400 (Rev 07/17/91)N

Part 9. Memberships and organizations.

A. List your present and past membership in or affiliation with every organization, association, fund, foundation, party, club, society, or similar group in the United States or in any other place. Include any military service in this part. If none, write "none". Include the name of organization, location, dates of membership and the nature of the organization. If additional space is needed, use separate paper.

_____

_____

_____

_____

Part 10. Complete only if you checked block " C " in Part 2.

How many of your parents are U.S. citizens? ☐ One   ☐ Both   (Give the following about one U.S. citizen parent:)

Family Name	Given Name	Middle Name

Address _____

Basis for citizenship:
☐ Birth
☐ Naturalization Cert. No.

Relationship to you (check one): ☐ natural parent   ☐ adoptive parent
☐ parent of child legitimated after birth

If adopted or legitimated after birth, give date of adoption or, legitimation: _(month/day/year)_ _____

Does this parent have legal custody of you? ☐ Yes   ☐ No

(Attach a copy of relating evidence to establish that you are the child of this U.S. citizen and evidence of this parent's citizenship.)

Part 11. Signature. _(Read the information on penalties in the instructions before completing this section)._

I certify or, if outside the United States, I swear or affirm under penalty of perjury under the laws of the United States of America that this application, and the evidence submitted with it, is all true and correct. I authorize the release of any information from my records which the Immigration and Naturalization Service needs to determine eligibility for the benefit I am seeking.

Signature _____   Date _____

Please Note: If you do not completely fill out this form, or fail to submit required documents listed in the instructions, you may not be found eligible for naturalization and this application may be denied.

Part 12. Signature of person preparing form if other than above. _(Sign below)_

I declare that I prepared this application at the request of the above person and it is based on all information of which I have knowledge.

Signature	Print Your Name	Date

Firm Name
and Address _____

DO NOT COMPLETE THE FOLLOWING UNTIL INSTRUCTED TO DO SO AT THE INTERVIEW

I swear that I know the contents of this application, and supplemental pages 1 through_____, that the corrections , numbered 1 through_____, were made at my request, and that this amended application, is true to the best of my knowledge and belief.

_____
(Complete and true signature of applicant)

Subscribed and sworn to before me by the applicant.

_____
(Examiner's Signature)   Date

*U.S. Government Printing Office: 1992 — 316-475/591

Form N-400 (Rev 07/17/91)N

U. S. IMMIGRATION & NATURALIZATION SERVICE

COLOR PHOTOGRAPH SPECIFICATIONS

IDEAL PHOTOGRAPH ◄

IMAGE MUST FIT INSIDE THIS BOX ►

THE PICTURE AT LEFT IS IDEAL SIZE, COLOR, BACKGROUND, AND POSE. THE IMAGE SHOULD BE 30MM (1 3/16IN) FROM THE HAIR TO JUST BELOW THE CHIN, AND 26MM (1 IN) FROM LEFT CHEEK TO RIGHT EAR. THE IMAGE MUST FIT IN THE BOX AT RIGHT.

THE PHOTOGRAPH

* THE OVERALL SIZE OF THE PICTURE, INCLUDING THE BACKGROUND, MUST BE AT LEAST 40MM (1 9/16 INCHES) IN HEIGHT BY 35MM (1 3/8IN) IN WIDTH.

* PHOTOS MUST BE FREE OF SHADOWS AND CONTAIN NO MARKS, SPLOTCHES, OR DISCOLORATIONS.

* PHOTOS SHOULD BE HIGH QUALITY, WITH GOOD BACK LIGHTING OR WRAP AROUND LIGHTING, AND MUST HAVE A WHITE OR OFF-WHITE BACKGROUND.

* PHOTOS MUST BE A GLOSSY OR MATTE FINISH AND UN-RETOUCHED.

* POLAROID FILM HYBRID #5 IS ACCEPTABLE; HOWEVER SX-70 TYPE FILM OR ANY OTHER INSTANT PROCESSING TYPE FILM IS UNACCEPTABLE. NON-PEEL APART FILMS ARE EASILY RECOGNIZED BECAUSE THE BACK OF THE FILM IS BLACK. ACCEPTABLE INSTANT COLOR FILM HAS A GRAY-TONED BACKING.

THE IMAGE OF THE PERSON

* THE DIMENSIONS OF THE IMAGE SHOULD BE 30MM (1 3/16 INCHES) FROM THE HAIR TO THE NECK JUST BELOW THE CHIN, AND 26MM (1 INCH) FROM THE RIGHT EAR TO THE LEFT CHEEK. IMAGE CANNOT EXCEED 32MM BY 28MM (1 1/4IN X 1 1/16IN).

* IF THE IMAGE AREA ON THE PHOTOGRAPH IS TOO LARGE OR TOO SMALL, THE PHOTO CANNOT BE USED.

* PHOTOGRAPHS MUST SHOW THE ENTIRE FACE OF THE PERSON IN A 3/4 VIEW SHOWING THE RIGHT EAR AND LEFT EYE.

* FACIAL FEATURES **MUST BE IDENTIFIABLE.**

* CONTRAST BETWEEN THE IMAGE AND BACKGROUND IS ESSENTIAL. PHOTOS FOR VERY LIGHT SKINNED PEOPLE SHOULD BE SLIGHTLY UNDER-EXPOSED. PHOTOS FOR VERY DARK SKINNED PEOPLE SHOULD BE SLIGHTLY OVER-EXPOSED.

SAMPLES OF UNACCEPTABLE PHOTOGRAPHS

INCORRECT POSE

IMAGE TOO LARGE

IMAGE TOO SMALL

IMAGE TOO DARK UNDER-EXPOSED

IMAGE TOO LIGHT

DARK BACKGROUND

OVER-EXPOSED

SHADOWS ON PIC

Immigration & Naturalization Service
Form M-378 (6-92)

Sample Fingerprint Chart

TYPE OR PRINT ALL INFORMATION IN BLACK   LEAVE BLANK

LAST NAME NAM   FIRST NAME   MIDDLE NAME

APPLICANT

SIGNATURE OF PERSON FINGERPRINTED	ALIASES AKA

O
R
I

NJINSNK00
USINS
NEWARK, NJ

RESIDENCE OF PERSON FINGERPRINTED

DATE OF BIRTH DOB
Month   Day   Year

CITIZENSHIP CTZ	SEX	RACE	HGT.	WGT.	EYES	HAIR	PLACE OF BIRTH POB

DATE	SIGNATURE OF OFFICIAL TAKING FINGERPRINTS

YOUR NO. OCA

LEAVE BLANK

EMPLOYER AND ADDRESS

FBI NO. FBI

CLASS _____

ARMED FORCES NO. MNU

REASON FINGERPRINTED

SOCIAL SECURITY NO. SOC

REF. _____

MISCELLANEOUS NO. MNU

1. R. THUMB	2. R. INDEX	3. R. MIDDLE	4. R. RING	5. R. LITTLE

6. L. THUMB	7. L. INDEX	8. L. MIDDLE	9. L. RING	10. L. LITTLE

LEFT FOUR FINGERS TAKEN SIMULTANEOUSLY	L. THUMB	R. THUMB	RIGHT FOUR FINGERS TAKEN SIMULTANEOUSLY

This page intentionally left blank

Use for notes

14 IMMIGRATION & NATURALIZATION SERVICE ADDRESSES

Written correspondence should be sent to: Immigration and Naturalization Service, followed by appropriate address from the list below

ALASKA
New Federal Bldg.
620 East 10th Ave, Rm. 102
Anchorage, Alaska 99501
Tel.# 907 271 3101/-3521

ARIZONA
Federal Bldg.
2035 North Central Ave.
Phoenix, Arizona 85004
Tel.# 602 379 6666/-3114

Federal Bldg.
300 West Congress , Rm 1-T
Tucson, Arizona 85701
Tel. # 602 629 6229

CALIFORNIA
Federal Bldg.
Room 1308,1130 O St.
Fresno, California 93721
Tel.# 209 487 5091/5646

Federal Bldg.
300 N. Los Angeles St.
Los Angeles, California 90012
Tel. # 213 894 6000/-2780

711 "J" Street
Sacramento, California 95814
Tel.# 916 551 3116

U.S. Federal Bldg.
880 Front Street, Rm. 2246
San Diego, California 92101-8834
Tel.# 619 557 5570/-5645

Appraisers Bldg.
630 Sansome St., Rm. 232
San Francisco, California 94111
Tel.# 415 705 4411/-4571

Federal Bldg.
280 South First St., Rm. 1150
San Jose, California 95113
Tel. # 408 291 7876

14560 Magnolia Street
Westminster, California 92683
No # given

COLORADO
Albrecht Center
4730 Paris Street
Denver, Colorado 80239
Tel.# 303 371 3041/-0986

CONNECTICUT
Abraham Ribicoff Federal Bldg.
450 Main St., Rm. 410
Hartford, Connecticut 06103-3060
Tel.# 203 240 3050

DISTRICT OF COLUMBIA
(Washington, DC)
4420 North Fairfax Dr., Rm. 210
Arlington, Virginia 22203
Tel.# 202 307 1501/-1640

FLORIDA
Post Office Bldg.
400 West Bay St. , Rm. G-18
Jacksonville, Florida 32202
Tel.# 904 791 2624/-3156

7880 Biscayne Blvd.
Miami, Florida 33138
Tel. # 305 530 7657/-7658
Florida continued next page

4 East Port Rd., Rm. 129
Riviera Beach, Florida 33404
Tel.# 305 844 4341

5509 West Gray St., Suite 113
Tampa, Florida 33609-1059
Tel.# 813 228 2131

GEORGIA
Dr. Martin Luther King, Jr. Federal Bldg.
77 Forsyth Street, SW- Rm. 117
Atlanta, Georgia 30303
Tel.# 404 331 0301/-5945

GUAM
801 Pacific News Bldg.
238 O'Hara Street
Agana, Guam 96910
Tel.# 671 472 6411

HAWAII
595 Ala Moana Blvd.
PO Box 461
Honolulu, Hawaii 96813
Tel.# 808 541 1388/-5220

IDAHO
4620 Overland Rd., Rm. 108
Boise, Idaho 83705
Tel.# 208 334 1821

ILLINOIS
10 West Jackson Blvd., Suite 600
Chicago, Illinois 60604
Tel.# 312 353 7302/-886-0600

INDIANA
Gateway Plaza, Rm. 400
950 North Meridian St.
Indianapolis, Indiana 46204
Tel.# 317 226 6009

KENTUCKY
U.S. Courthouse Bldg.
West 6th & Broadway., #601
Louisville, Kentucky 40202
Tel.# 502 582 6375

LOUISIANA
Postal Service Bldg., Rm. T-8011
701 Loyola Ave.
New Orleans, Louisiana 70113
Tel.# 504 589 6532/-6535/-6521

MAINE
739 Warren Avenue, Rm. 316
Portland, Maine 04103
Tel.# 207 780 3352/-3399

MARYLAND
100 S. Charles St., 12th Fl.
Equitable Center One
Baltimore, Maryland 21201
Tel.# 301 962 2120/-2010

MASSA-CHUSETTS
John F. Kennedy Federal Office Bldg.
Government Center, Rm. 700
Boston, Massachusetts 02203
Tel.# 617 565 4214

MICHIGAN
Federal Building, INS
333 Mount Elliott St.
Detroit, Michigan 48207-4381
Tel.# 313 568 6000

MINNESOTA
2901 Metro Drive, Suite 100
Bloomington, Minnesota 55425
Tel.# 612 335 2211

MISSOURI
9747 North Conant Ave.
Kansas City, Missouri 64153
Tel.# 816 891 9318/-9312/-9314

1222 Spruce Street, Suite 1100
St. Louis, Missouri 63103-2815
Tel. # 314 539 2532

MONTANA
Federal Bldg., Drawer 10036
301 South Park, Room 512
Helena, Montana 59626-0036
Tel.# 406 449 5288/-5220

NEBRASKA
3736 South 132nd St.
Omaha, Nebraska 68144
Tel.# 402 697 9152

NEVADA
Federal Bldg.
300 Las Vegas Blvd. S., Rm. 104
Las Vegas, Nevada 89101
Tel.# 702 384 3696

350 S. Rock Boulevard
Reno, Nevada 89502
Tel. # 702 784 5644

NEW JERSEY
Federal Bldg.
970 Broad St.
Newark, New Jersey 07102
Tel.# 201 645 4400/-2269

NEW MEXICO
517 Gold Ave. SW, Rm. 1114
Albuquerque, New Mexico 87103
Tel.# 505 766 2378

NEW YORK
Post Office & Courthouse Bldg.
445 Broadway, Room 220
Albany, New York 12207
Tel.# 518 472 7140

130 Delaware Ave
Buffalo, New York 14202
Tel. # 716 846 4741/-6760

Jacob Javits Federal Bldg.
26 Federal Plaza, Rm. 14-102
New York, New York 10278
Tel.# 212 264 5942/-5944
Fax: 212 264 5939

NORTH CAROLINA
6 Woodlawn Green, Suite 138
Charlotte, North Carolina 28217
Tel.# 704 523 1704/-344-6331

OHIO
J.W. Peck Federal Bldg.
550 Main St., Rm. 8525
Cincinnati, Ohio 45201
Tel.# 513 684 2930

A.J. Celebreeze Federal Office Bldg.
1240 E. 9th St., Rm. 1917
Cleveland, Ohio 44199
Tel. # 216 522 4767

OKLAHOMA
4149 Highline Blvd., Suite 300
Oklahoma City, Oklahoma 73108
Tel.# 405 942 8670

OREGON
Federal Office Bldg.
511 NW Broadway
Portland, Oregon 97209
Tel.# 503 326 2271/-3962

PENNSYLVANIA	16th & Callowhill Sts. **Philadelphia**, Pennsylvania 19130 Tel.# 215 656 7150	Federal Bldg. 1000 Liberty Ave. **Pittsburgh**, Pennsylvania 15222 Tel.# 412 644 3356
PUERTO RICO	Federal Bldg., Rm. 380 Chardon Avenue **Hato Rey**, Puerto Rico 00936 or PO Box 365063 **San Juan**, Puerto Rico 00936 Tel.# 809 766 7479/-5380/-5329	
RHODE ISLAND	Pastore Federal Bldg., Room 203 **Providence**, Rhode Island 02903 Tel.# 401 454 7440	
SOUTH CAROLINA	Federal Bldg., Room 110 334 Meeting St. **Charleston**, South Carolina 29403 Tel.# 803 727 4350/-4422/-4359	
TENNESSEE	245 Wagner Place, Rm. 250 **Memphis**, Tennessee 38103 Tel.# 901 544 3301/-4056	
TEXAS	Federal Bldg. 8101 N. Stemmons Freeway **Dallas**, Texas 75247 Tel.# 214 655 3011	700 East Antonio PO Box 9398 **El Paso**, Texas 79984 Tel. # 915 534 6366/-6334
	2102 Teege Road **Harlingen**, Texas 78550 Tel.# 512 425 7342/-8592	509 North Belt (Main Floor) **Houston**, Texas 77060 Tel. # 713 847 7960
	8940 Fourwinds **San Antonio**, Texas 78239 Tel.# 210 871 7072	
U.S. VIRGIN ISLANDS	PO Box 1270 Kingshill, Christiansted **St. Croix**, U.S. V. I. 00850 Tel.# 809 773 7559	Federal Bldg. ,PO Box 629 Charlotte Amalie **St. Thomas**, U.S. VI 00801 Tel. # 809 774 1390
UTAH	230 West 400 South St. **Salt Lake City**, Utah 84101 Tel.# 801 524 6272	
VERMONT	Federal Bldg. 50 South Main St., PO Box 328 **St. Albans**, Vermont 05478 Tel.# 802 524 6742	
VIRGINIA	Norfolk Federal Bldg. 200 Granby Mall, Rm. 439 **Norfolk**, Virginia 23510 Tel.# 804 441 3081/-3095	

WASHINGTON   815 Airport Way South   691 U. S. Federal Courthouse Bldg.
                    Seattle, Washington 98134   West 920 Riverside
                    Tel.# 206 553 5956/-0070   **Spokane**, Washington 99201

WISCONSIN   Federal Bldg., Rm. 186
                    517 East Wisconsin Ave.
                    Milwaukee, Wisconsin 53202
                    Tel.# 414 291 3565/-3161

FOREIGN OFFICES

Bangkok, **Thailand**   Mexico City, **Mexico**
c/o American Embassy   c/o American Embassy
APO AE 96546   PO Box 3087, Rm. 118
(011) (66) (2) 252 5040 x2614   Laredo, TX 78044
                                        (011) (525) 211 0042 x3514

Rome, **Italy**
c/o American Embassy
PSC 59, Box 100
APO AE 09624
(011) (39) (6) 467 4239 x2572

INS HEADQUARTERS

425 "I" Street, NW
Washington, DC 20536
Tel.# 202 514 4330

There are no INS offices in the following states. Contact the INS office in parentheses for further information.

ALABAMA (Atlanta, Georgia)
ARKANSAS (New Orleans, Louisiana)
DELAWARE (Philadelphia, Pennsylvania)
IOWA (Omaha, Nebraska)
KANSAS (Kansas City, Missouri)
MISSISSIPPI (New Orleans, Louisiana)
NEW HAMPSHIRE (Boston, Massachusetts)
NORTH DAKOTA (Bloomington, Minnesota)
SOUTH DAKOTA (Bloomington, Minnesota)
WEST VIRGINIA (Philadelphia, Pennsylvania)
WYOMING (Denver, Colorado)

There are also four Regional Service Centers located throughout the U.S., which process several of the routine nonimmigrant and immigrant visa petitions. Their addresses are:

✍ **Vermont Service Center**
(formerly Eastern Regional Service Center)
75 Lower Welden Street
St. Albans, **Vermont** 05479-0001
Tel. # 802 527 3160
This office has jurisdiction over the following states: MA, CT, NH, RI, NY, PA, DE, WV, MD, NJ, DC, VA, ME, VT and also over the INS offices in: Puerto Rico, Bermuda, Toronto, Montreal, Virgin Islands and Dominican Republic

✍ **Nebraska Service Center**
(formerly Northern Regional Service Center)
850 "S" Street
Lincoln, **Nebraska** 68501
Tel. # 402 437 5218/-5464
FAX: 402 437 5205
This office has jurisdiction over the following states: MI, IL, IN, WI, OR, AK, MN, ND, SD, KS, MO, WA, ID, CO, UT, WY, OH, NE, IA, and also over the INS offices in: Manitoba, British Columbia and Calgary

✍ **Texas Service Center**
(formerly Southern Regional Service Center)
PO Box 15122
Dept. "A"
Irving, **Texas** 75015-2122
Tel. # 214 767 7769
This office has jurisdiction over the following states: FL, TX, NM, OK, GA, NC, SC, AL, LA, AR, MS, TN, KY, and also over the INS offices in: Bahamas, Freeport and Nassau

✍ **California Service Center**
(formerly Western Regional Service Center)
for expedite and courier deliveries
24000 Avila Road, 2nd Fl, Rm. 2304
Laguna Niguel, **California** 92677
Attn: Incoming Mailroom

for regular mail
PO Box 30111
Laguna Niguel, CA 926770-8011
This office has jurisdiction over the following states: CA, HI, AZ, NV and Guam

Note: many states have more than one Immigration Office. If you have a deadline, or need to save time, telephone the INS office to confirm whether the application that you are filing is being mailed to the appropriate address, or whether it should be sent to a Regional Service Center.

15 United States Passport Agencies

Boston
John F. Kennedy Building,
Government Center, Room E123,
Boston, MA 02203
(617) 565-3940

Chicago
Kluczynski Federal Office Building
230 S. Dearborn, Suite 380
Chicago, IL 60604
(312) 353-5426

Honolulu
New Federal Building
300 Ala Moana Blvd.-Room C-06
Honolulu, HI 96850
(808) 546-2130

Houston
One Allen Center
500 Dallas St.
Houston, TX 77002
(713) 229-3607

Los Angeles
Federal Building
11000 Wilshire Blvd.-Room 13100
West Los Angeles, CA 90024
(213) 209-7070

Miami
Federal Office Building
51 SW 1st Ave.-16th Floor
Miami, FL 33130
(305) 536-5395

continued on next page

New Orleans
Postal Service Building
701 Loyola Ave.- Room Y-12005
New Orleans, LA 70113
(504) 589-6728

New York City
630 Fifth Ave.-Room 270
New York, NY 10111
(212) 541-7700

Philadelphia
Federal Office Building
600 Arch St.-Room 4426
Philadelphia, PA 19106
(215) 597-7480

San Francisco
525 Market St., Suite 200
San Francisco, CA 94105
(415) 974-7972

Seattle
Federal Office Building
915 Second Ave.-Room 992
Seattle, WA 98174
(206) 325-3538

Stamford
One Landmark Square
Broad and Atlantic Sts.
Stamford, CT 06901
(203) 325-3538

Washington, DC
1425 K St., NW
Washington, DC 20524
(202) 523-1355

Index

USE THIS FORM IF THIS BOOK IS NOT AVAILABLE AT YOUR LOCAL BOOKSTORE

Order Form

SHIP TO:

YOUR NAME AND TITLE:_____

NAME OF ORGANIZATION: _____

STREET ADDRESS: _____

CITY:_____STATE:_____ZIP: _____

TELEPHONE: _____

Please send the following:

_____copies of Citizenship Made Simple at $15.95 per book

_____copies of Immigration Made Simple at $18.95 per book

Shipping charges: $4.00 for first book, $1.00 for each additional book.

A check for $_____ is enclosed.

Orders must be prepaid unless using an official purchase order.

Mail to:

**Next Decade, Inc.
39 Old Farmstead Road
Chester, NJ 07930
Telephone/Fax: (908) 879-6625**

FISHWHEELS
OF THE
COLUMBIA

FISHWHEELS

OF THE

COLUMBIA

by

Ivan J. Donaldson and Frederick K. Cramer

BINFORDS & MORT, *Publishers*

Portland   •   Oregon   •   97242

DEDICATION

To the fishwheel men of the Columbia River whose
ingenious salmon wheels churned the turbulent waters
of that great stream during one of the most colorful
epochs in the history of the river.

Fishwheels of the Columbia

COPYRIGHT UNDER INTERNATIONAL
PAN-AMERICAN COPYRIGHT CONVENTION
COPYRIGHT © 1971 BY BINFORDS & MORT, PUBLISHERS

ALL RIGHTS RESERVED INCLUDING THE RIGHT
TO REPRODUCE THIS BOOK, OR ANY PORTIONS
THEREOF, IN ANY FORM EXCEPT FOR THE IN-
CLUSION OF BRIEF QUOTATIONS IN A REVIEW.

LIBRARY OF CONGRESS CATALOG CARD NUMBER: 76-173928
ISBN: 0-8323-0007-1

Printed in the United States of America

FIRST EDITION

INTRODUCTION

Fishwheels were one of the most ingenious devices ever invented for capturing fish. Strategically located in swift water in the pathways of migrating fish, these wheels used the flowing waters to catch and deposit the fish with a minimum of human effort. Depending on water current alone for power, their efficient operation has never been equaled by any other fishing method.

Though not introduced on the Columbia River until 1879, such wheels were common on the east coast of the United States as early as 1829, notably in the shad fisheries on the Pee Dee and Roanoke rivers of North Carolina. However, the most concentrated assemblage of fishwheels for commercial purposes was on the Columbia River, particularly at two main locations—the area of swift water at The Cascades, where the river courses between Skamania and Multnomah counties, and the region from The Dalles to Celilo Falls, between Klickitat and Wasco counties.

While the number of fishwheels varied from year to year, at least 76 were in use on the river in 1899. The wheels operated for nearly half a century until finally prohibited by law, in 1926 in Oregon and in 1934 in Washington.

Fortunately, when the authors decided to record the story of the Columbia River fishwheels—a thing which no historian had yet attempted—a few wheel men with excellent memories still remained to give a portion of it, along with many personal recollections of fishwheel experience. Both authors — Ivan Donaldson who researched the Cascade region and Frederick Cramer who researched The Dalles-Celilo area—learned much from these men who had spent their lives on the river. Largely through their help, *Fishwheels of the Columbia* preserves a way of life that otherwise would probably have been lost forever.

Francis and Ed Seufert, Earnest Cramer, Chris Kitto, Chris Peterson, Jack Johnson, Hans Blaser, and Walter Klindt of The Dalles, Oregon; C. W. Cleland of Vancouver, Washington; William and Fred Sams of Skamania, Washington; and Eric Enquist of Fairview, Oregon — all gave unstintingly of time and information during preparation of this book. Friends exhumed long-forgotten fishwheel photographs from their albums. Personnel of the Oregon Room, at the University of Oregon Library, and the Oregon Historical Society contributed photographs and documentary data. Mrs. Nancy Hacker spent countless hours in the Library of Congress checking the authors' notes.

When the Portland *Oregonian* printed an appeal for fishwheel material and pictures, Mrs. J. F. McCord generously responded. Dr. James H. Huddleson sent a rare 1890 photograph of one of the first scow wheels on the river. Mrs. Dorothy P. Nile, who lived a number of childhood years at Cascade Locks, supplied excellent views of early days there. Also in response to the article, Mrs. Frank Swick of Ridgefield, Washington, sent a photograph of her uncle, Samuel Wilson, builder of the first "rotary fishing machine" on the river.

The authors are grateful to Lois Leonard, who persuaded them to do more than "report"; to Clyde Archibald, fishway designer, Corps of Engineers, for his technical information; and to Mrs. Winona Ritchey, librarian, Oregon Fish Commission at Clackamas. Many others also contributed, to all of whom the authors extend deep appreciation.

CONTENTS

PART ONE

THE CASCADE REGION

PART TWO

THE DALLES-CELILO REGION

PART ONE

THE CASCADE REGION

Moffett Creek Wheel on Moffett Creek Bar, showing excellent craftsmanship and finish by Warren's fishwheel crew. Hamilton Island is across river. (Oregon Historical Society)

THE ORIGIN OF FISHWHEELS

From their first appearance on the Columbia River in 1879, fishwheels aroused the deep hatred of net fishermen and sharp jealousies among operators of the wheels themselves, resulting in some of the bitterest and greediest battles in the history of any fishery. Although the wheels captured only 5 to 7 per cent of the total commercial harvest of Columbia salmon, they were the most ingenious, picturesque, and controversial devices ever designed to catch fish.

Strategically located in the pathways of migrating fish, the wheels used the swift-flowing waters to catch, and deposit in a pen, migrant salmon and other fish with a minimum of human effort. The vast power of the river thrusting against the dippers of the wheels could lift several hundred pounds of fish free of the water—and on occasion tear giant sturgeon to pieces when they became jammed between the wheel and its supports.

British writer Rudyard Kipling saw them for the first time when he visited the Pacific Northwest in the summer of 1889. He described them as an "infernal arrangement of wire-gauze compartments worked by the current to scoop up the salmon as he races up the river," and again as "revolving cups of a giant wheel." His companion on the journey swore long and bluntly when told of the weight of a good night's catch—some thousands of pounds.

"Think of the black and bloody murder of it," he said. Apparently neither Kipling nor his companion chose to comment on the "black and bloody murder" caused by thousands of nets and hundreds of fixed traps also on the river.

Exactly when the first fishwheel in the world was constructed remains a mystery. Most likely it was a by-product of other construction work. It is generally believed that it evolved from some long-since-forgotten undershot water wheel—in which water flowing under the wheel turned it. A bucket wheel could easily have brought up fish along with the water. Ages ago—possibly in China, for irrigation there goes back many centuries—some farmer might have noticed that the buckets of his irrigation wheel lifted fish above the tailwater surface. From this point of origin, the idea could have traveled westward to the United States.

Though a few maintain that Alaska was the place of origin, this theory has been disproved. Fishwheels first appeared in Alaska in the late 1890s and early 1900s and were evidently introduced there by persons who had seen them used on the Columbia. This theory is supported by the Alaska Department of Fish and Game. The inflated sealskin used by the Eskimos as a roller is certainly not a wheel and there is a vast difference between the roller and the wheel with a fixed axle. Pre-Columbian Indians probably used the roller, but if they did know about the wheel they put it to no practical use, even in their pottery making.

Fishwheels were common in the shad fisheries on the East Coast of the United States as early as 1829—notably on the Roanoke and Pee Dee rivers of the Carolinas—but they were not introduced to the Columbia until 1879, when Samuel Wilson built his first fishwheel at the Cascades of the river. This was approximately fourteen years after commercial fishing began on the Columbia. Soon in these waters there developed the most concentrated assemblage of fishwheels for commercial purposes anywhere in the world — particularly at two locations: the area of swift water, on both sides of the river, at the Cascades; and the upriver region stretching from The Dalles to Celilo Falls. All told, these two areas comprised approximately 34 miles. While the number of wheels varied from year to year, at least 76 were operating on the river by the close of the century. And, it was on this river that the wheels reached their most sophisticated level of development.

Use of these wheels was prohibited by Oregon law in 1926, and by Washington law in 1934, and now even most vestiges of the old wheels are gone. Construction of Bonneville and The Dalles dams inundated most of them, with the structures themselves being torn down or burned during the reservoir-clearing operations prior to raising of the pools.

7

At other places they have either been removed or have fallen as a result of rotting timbers and natural elements, including high water. By 1960, only one wheel remained recognizable on the Columbia—the Phelps Wheel at Threemile Rapids, a few hundred feet upstream from the bridge at The Dalles, Oregon. Now it, too, is gone.

The most authentic account available on the origin of fishwheels is included in the records of the United States District Court of Oregon, Judgment No. 826. In prolonged and heated litigation, beginning January 12, 1882, and ending 26 months later, Thornton F. Williams of the Upper Cascades (now Cascade Locks), in Oregon, sought to stop William Rankin McCord and the Snail Wheel Fishing Company from infringing on his fishwheel patent, avowing that he had suffered damages of $100,000.

Evidence brought out at the trial, however, indicated that credit for invention of the wheels, in the United States at least, properly belonged to the brothers, William and Robert Thomas of Rockingham, North Carolina, who for many years prior to this had successfully operated "fish dippers" on the Pee Dee River. According to regional tradition they had introduced them into that area. One Stephen Cole, age 75 and president of the First National Bank of Salisbury, North Carolina, testified that he had known these men personally and had seen their operations. He said that he had been aware of such revolving dipnets or "dippers" on the river for "at least 50 years or more"—which would indicate the success of the Thomas brothers' invention. Cole stated:

"I have seen many such wheels extending from a point on the Pee Dee River at the Pegen fishery in South Carolina, where Sherman's army passed, and 100 miles upstream. Each dipper had three buckets over which netting was stretched. The fishing devices were made with three arms or dippers, 2½ to 3 feet wide extending from the axle 3½ to 5 feet, depending on the stream and depth of water. The ends of the dippers must nearly touch bottom to catch the fish . . . . The bows of the dippers were made of white oak or other tough wood. Slats were affixed across the bows for strength. Then netting of flax or cotton was stretched on the axle and bow frame. An inclined plane was provided in each dip to move the fish to a box located on a rock pile which held the forks, or stakes, in which the machine revolved."

By 1862, Wesley Pegen owned seven such revolving dippers on the Pee Dee River, but more than a hundred were then in existence, and all were located in "fast water" in a sluice or current. Slight or low dams were erected to create currents, and the nets were placed athwart the dam openings. On each side of the revolving nets, parallel stakes or posts were placed to support the revolving axle.

This four-dip wheel was shown in the May 1880 issue of Harper's Weekly, *illustrating the earliest known fishwheels in the United States, which were traced back to 1829 on the Roanoke and Pee Dee rivers of the Carolinas.*

"Herring fishing machine"—a Roanoke River catamaran-type fishwheel with only one scoop. (Jack Dermid)

Roanoke River catamaran fishwheel, North Carolina. Note fish falling into pontoon, and wooden axle. (Jack Dermid)

Thornton Williams fishwheel prior to 1889, and prior to remodeling by Frank Warren's crew. Note the workman near water level attaching salmon to a cask float which will carry the salmon down to the cannery at Warrendale. An angler can be seen fishing from the machine; this was not done following 1889, for some unknown reason. (Donald R. Munro)

FIRST WHEELS ON THE COLUMBIA

Thornton Williams, recently of Iowa but then living at the Cascades on the Columbia, had managed to secure the first patent on a fishwheel, No. 243,251, dated August 6, 1881. However, the year before, a man by the name of William Rankin McCord had visited the Cascades, viewed the flimsy Thornton Williams Wheel, and decided he could build a better one. Already an inventive blacksmith and violin maker, McCord set out to devise patentable improvements on the Thornton Williams machine.

With the aid of Frank Warren and the banker, William Sargent Ladd of Portland, in December, 1881, McCord began construction of a two-dip wheel on the south shore of Bradford Island—which island today forms a part of Bonneville Dam.

Frank Warren was a bright young man employed at Ladd & Tilton Bank when he met and impressed Ladd, the pioneer Portland banker. In 1876, Ladd gave Warren a new assignment; he was to rebuild a moribund fish-packing company in which the bank had heavy investments. Thus, Warren was on the scene when fishwheels first appeared on the Columbia, and he was astute enough to recognize their potential. After gaining a 99-year lease on Bradford Island, he was free to use the location to develop a fishing and boat-building center—which he proceeded to do with the help of McCord.

By early 1882 the men had constructed a wheel on the island—the third wheel on the river—at the approximate site where salmon now enter Bonneville Lake above the powerhouse. The patent trial had opened in January of that year, but there was plenty of profitable fishing to be derived from the turning wheels, and it would take a court injunction to stop them, as far as McCord and Warren were concerned.

McCord later recalled that one day a wheel took several thousand salmon, not counting small fish and steelheads; and one night his wheel caught thirty tons of sturgeon. Every dip of the paddle brought in two fish; these sturgeon he estimated would average 150 pounds each, and some weighed 500 pounds. In one 24-hour period, a catch of 10,000 salmon was recorded. No wonder fisheries sometimes worked around the clock. (Though there is

McCord's word for the numbers, the authors feel that, in this instance, imagination was also at work.)

The first McCord wheel had operated only a short time before the catch of salmon was so great that the dead weight of fish caused several structural timbers to collapse. No one could have foreseen this. The weight must have been tremendous. McCord's grandson, Aubrey Archer, recalled:

"One morning Grandfather McCord came down to the wheel to find it broken and stopped, with the scow beside it in nearly sinking condition from the salmon it held. Salmon piled up in the wheel until they prevented it from turning. They were jammed between it and the scow, which was barely afloat from the weight of the fish it contained."

The price for fish ran from 10 to 25 cents in the early 1880s. Small salmon and bluebacks sold for 3 cents apiece, and salmon in the neighborhood of 30 pounds brought 15 cents. A large chinook weighing 30 to 65 pounds, or more, could be purchased for 30 cents. And these were not prices per pound, but per fish.

On May 16, 1882, while the trial was going on, "McCord and Associates" were issued Patent No. 257,960 for an invention entitled "fishwheel." McCord was then 52 years of age, and his various inventions included development of the first scow wheel on the river. Some of the first stationaries had block and tackle "elevators" for adjustment of the dippers to the proper depth. Since fish would be lost upstream if water rose above the axle, it was customary to set wheels with their axles several feet above the river surface. But there were periods of low and very high water when the stationary wheels could not be fished. To the early fishery tycoon this was an intolerable situation, and the ingenious McCord "did something about it." He developed the first scow wheel.

Litigation of patent rights continued until March 26, 1884. During the power struggle many confusing statements were made. Thornton Williams claimed that he had begun his first wheel on October 14, 1878, and had completed it in August 1879. However, what finally seemed to swing the outcome of the trial away from Williams was the testimony of James Parker, a farmer and fisherman

Samuel Wilson and family. (Carrie Swick)

who appeared to have no personal motives involved in the verdict and nothing to gain.

In sworn testimony, James Parker stated that the Thornton Williams Wheel was nearly the same as the unpatented wheel erected by Samuel Wilson early in 1879 on the Washington side of the river at a site just below Fort Rains. Wilson's structure was a rather small, insecure, two-dip, stake-type wheel with no "leads"—that is, no artificial channel or fence to lead the fish into the dippers. Furthermore, he, James Parker, had shown Thornton Williams this wheel and told him how Samuel Wilson intended to improve it.

"Thornton Williams came three or four times on different days to look at Samuel Wilson's wheel while it was running," Parker testified, stating that he personally had fished the Wilson machine until the 1879 spring freshet broke it up and carried it away. He recalled:

"I caught about two barrels of fish in it. Wilson left it in my charge when he returned to Iowa. . . . Neither Wilson nor his wife were healthy and they left for health reasons. . . . At the time I was running Wilson's wheel, Thornton Williams was fishing with a dipnet. That was all he was doing at the time. . . . The fall after Wilson's wheel went out, Thornton Williams commenced to build his wheel."

As it turned out, neither Samuel Wilson nor Thornton Williams nor William Rankin McCord could claim invention of the fishwheel. The presiding judge, Matthew P. Deady—reasoning from the Pee Dee dippers of the 1830s and 1840s—decided that, because similar wheels had been used for decades, they had become public property, hence were not patentable. However, he also decreed that, in 1879, at the age of 34, Samuel Wilson was the first individual to erect a revolving dipnet or fishwheel on the Columbia. No proof had been brought forward to support Thornton Williams' claim of a wheel begun in October of 1878.

Above: *The early Williams wheel looking into downstream side of dipway, about 1883. Note there is no outboard wall of fishwheel. (Donald R. Munro)*

Top right: *Thornton Williams fishwheel showing Government Slide (part of Cascade Slide) across river.*

The Thornton Williams fishwheel showing closer view of the hexagonal Chinese webbing obtained from San Francisco, about 1883. (Donald R. Munro)

13

Frank Manley Warren about 1910—fishwheel pioneer of the Cascades. (Oregon Historical Society)

View of Warren's Cannery from Mosquito Island, showing China house to the left and boat launching incline to the right of the cannery. An old unknown scow fishwheel lead can be seen on the bank in front of Ira Dodson's orchard, about 1901. (Kiser Bros.)

"WARREN'S SWEDES"

Today, precious few of the old wheel men who fished the then-racing waters at the Cascades are available to tell about it. Of those interviewed, Eric Enquist had the most experience and personal interest. He arrived in the United States, June 2, 1902, an emigrant from a community of Swedes in Finland. Within a few days he headed for the Pacific Northwest, having heard good reports about fishing conditions on the Columbia River. While traveling along the river, he observed and was greatly intrigued by the huge wheels in action.

On reaching Portland, inquiry led him to Frank Warren, and Eric soon became one of "Warren's Swedes." He was assigned as tender for three years to Scow Wheel No. 2, at what is now Bonneville Dam's navigation lock site. While there he learned to read and write English by studying the Portland *Oregonian* in conjunction with a dictionary. He recalled:

"I have been interested in fishwheels from the first time I saw them. My country people, the Finland Swedes, had made a good name for themselves with Frank Warren. The June freshet was up; many salmon were running, and Warren needed extra men to help on the wheels. Consequently, I got a job there. . . . When I started building and operating my own fishwheels I had Joseph Latourell, a pioneer of 1852, to tend my wheels. He was not a fishwheel man personally, but he built what he called a schooner, rigged it with sails, and used it to transport wood from the section around Stevenson, Washington, to The Dalles."

Eric Enquist and family at McCord Wheel, about 1910. Scow 2 is visible across Bradford Slough on the Oregon shore. (Eric Enquist)

Fish on floor of Warren's Cannery, collected from his various wheels. This picture was taken in 1902, which was after *the great abundance of salmon harvest in the 1880s. (William Sams, II)*

Another interesting wheel man was Ed Nieman. While en route west by train about 1885, he by chance became acquainted with Frank Warren, who induced him to join the Warren organization. In a short while, Nieman became construction superintendent of the Warren operations. He pioneered many improvements in their enterprise at the Cascades, where he became known as an expert.

Nieman was a short man of about five feet and weighed around 150 pounds, in contrast to the typically Swedish crew he supervised, who were all men of large physical stature and capable of performing tasks requiring much strength. This contrast resulted in an amusing incident about 1890. A heavy 4-inch wheel axle, 12 feet long plus flanges, had been unloaded from the train onto the shore oppo-

site Bradford Island. Having no horses or automotive equipment at hand, the mighty Swedes were forced to carry this exceedingly heavy shaft 400 feet to the river and load it onto a boat for transport to the island. As the weight shifted and the men buckled under the burden, it was amusing to see little Ed Nieman trotting along under the axle, arms raised over his head, supposedly helping his crew support the load.

After the early Warren machines were swept away by the flood of 1894, the ability and experience of the Swedes in constructing strong log houses was put to use to rebuild the fishwheels. They used heavy cribworks of logs filled with hundreds of tons of rocks to make sturdy foundations.

Not a man for figures, Superintendent Nieman left the bookkeeping up to Ed Cook, but once when the latter made a serious mistake, Nieman hastened to Portland to relate the story to Warren before anyone else could reach the "boss." However, Nieman's energy and loyalty kept him in Warren's favor. Warren even presented him with a fine new suit of clothes when he left Bradford Island in 1900 to visit his native Norway. He died there in 1938, never returning to the Columbia Gorge as he had planned. Joel Westerlund succeeded him as Warren's construction superintendent, holding this position until the end of the wheel era.

Frank Warren died in 1912, a victim of the *Titanic* disaster, when on that fateful night of April 14-15, the "unsinkable" liner crashed into an iceberg in the North Atlantic south of Newfoundland. Among members of the Warren family, stories are still told of the chaos existing when the woefully inadequate lifeboats were launched, how Frank Warren embraced Mrs. Warren, bidding her a last farewell, and then calmly stepped back on the listing deck as the women and children were lowered to the sea. In the darkness of the cold night, Mrs. Warren could not see her husband as she looked back, and he was not among the survivors brought to New York by the *Carpathia*.

Following the tragedy, Warren's sons assumed leadership of the Warren organization. The cannery at Warrendale ceased operation about 1930 and later, about 1933, the government purchased Bradford Island and other holdings to build Bonneville Dam. After that the fishing company was formally dissolved.

Thornton Williams, the wily claimant of the first fishwheel patent—who went to court to "protect" the patent from infringement by William Rankin McCord—was never heard of again at the Cascades after he joined the gold rush to Alaska in 1898, except for a story told by the son of one of the participants. Reportedly he was seen attempting an escape from a threatened lynching by a party of Portland and Cascade Locks gold seekers whom he had lured north with promises that he knew the location of a fabulous ore bed.

And Samuel Wilson—credited by court of law with the first fishwheel on the Columbia—had returned in 1879 to his Iowa farm. The water had been too low after completion of his wheel to test its efficiency; that job was left to James Parker. Wilson never returned to the Columbia and quite possibly never learned of the distinction accorded him by Judge Deady at the conclusion of the trial.

The Thornton Williams fishwheel as rebuilt by Warren's crew following the 1894 flood.
Government Slide shows across the river. (Oregon Historical Society)

THE DODSON WHEELS

As far as can be determined, Frank Warren established his cannery in 1876 or 1877, on land originally owned by Ira Dodson. Because Sarah, Dodson's wife, refused to sign the deed of sale, Dodson could give Warren only a 99-year lease to the 40 acres east of his main holding; but Warren subsequently gained unrestricted ownership of the property.

Ira Dodson, an old-timer of the Columbia River Gorge, once owned all the shore land from the Myron B. Kelly line, a quarter mile west of McCord Creek, downstream two miles to the Robert Reed property. Here, six miles west of Bradford Island, he erected a store and dock. He employed a crew of Chinese to cut cordwood for the boilers of the regal sternwheelers that tied up at his place. All his wood-sale activity, though, had passed into history by 1889.

Dodson noted the success of the Williams Wheel and set about to construct a similar device. At the patent trial, H. T. Wood, who was familiar with the early South Carolina fishwheels, testified that he

Ira Dodson's lower wheel, 1903. Photo was taken from opposite McGowan's Cannery. Aldrich Butte shows on the left. (Kiser Bros.)

had seen the Williams Wheel and had helped build one for Dodson. William Rankin McCord testified in July that Thomas Robinson of East Portland constructed a wheel for Dodson, identical to the one belonging to Thornton Williams. It would seem that both of Dodson's dippers were completed prior to May 1883. Both withstood the ravages of the 1894 flood. About 1890, Dodson sold a portion of his holdings to Sam Gorman, but reserved the fishing rights.

Dodson's lower wheel was situated near the old, so-called Dodson railroad siding. The remaining pile of rocks that once filled the log cribbing has since served as a mount for a navigation light. The upper wheel, of the same standard size and crib-type construction, was located three-fourths mile farther upriver. No one knows which was built first. Each was placed above eddies, with conventional inboard and outboard fish-diverter fences or leads. Leads on the upper wheel were about 75 feet long, and those on the lower were 110 feet near the shore, and approximately 100 feet in an outboard direction. The outside lead piling were driven, whereas the inside ones were hand set.

The pick-up boat from Warren's Cannery came for Dodson's fish each day, and the catch from both wheels was usually mediocre.

Dodson operated his wheels until his divorce from Sarah. In the property settlement, Sarah gained possession of the wheels and all the land remaining. Oregon Fish Commission records list her as a wheel licensee for many years. She and her son, Hiram, fished the wheels until she (age 79 or 80) married Bill Broadback, a Swiss about half her age, who then took over the operation. After Sarah died in 1921, a legal agreement gave Hiram the Portland real estate and half the cash, while Broadback was awarded the two wheels, residual money, and all river frontage.

Soon thereafter, Douglas Lively paid Broadback a moderate fee for the wheels and acreage. With this Broadback vacationed in Switzerland for several months. On his return he had only $30, most of which he used for taxi fare to travel back out to Warrendale. There his trail ends. Douglas Lively, a man of varied endeavors who succeeded him, operated the wheels until 1927. Thereafter the timbers rotted away, leaving only a pile of boulders.

The Warrendale Post Office at one time was located in Ira Dodson's store, and later in the Sam Gorman home just downstream from Dodson's upper wheel. Ironically, at another time it was situated in McGowan's Cannery, a competitive enterprise to that of Frank Warren, for whom the post office was named. No one seems to recall when the name Dodson finally settled on the community. Both areas are presently served by the Bonneville Post Office.

About 1890, Ira's son, Hiram, constructed a scow wheel lead off the upper end of Pierce (Mosquito) Island Bar, together with a saloon on the higher portion of the island. When the scow washed away in a spring freshet, he fashioned another lead about a thousand feet downstream; but sand filled in below this structure and he abandoned the shoreline if not the liquor house. A "thirsty" river swallowed the latter in the 1894 flood.

Earlier, Hiram had placed a scow wheel about 500 feet west of Warren's Cannery on the Oregon shore, of which only the piling stubs and remnants of horizontal bar leads could be seen in 1889. He used two-inch chicken wire inside the dips in addition to the heavy wire of larger mesh, and as a result, caught a few more jack salmon and blueback, as well as many more suckers—nuisance fish.

Several years after the younger Dodson forsook his Pierce Island fishing efforts, Rudolph Koch and Fred Ladzic built a long sea wall of piling and closely fitted 2x8-foot planks along the south shore of the island to protect the shoreline. They then installed a scow wheel with lead out from the breakwater, but it did not fish well because the lack of current at certain flows caused sand to fill in below the lead. This hand-placed fish-diverter started at the shearwater and extended about 75 or 100 feet into the river. It was made of driven piling on 6-foot centers, with the customary horizontal 2 x 4s nailed across the stakes.

Pierce Island consists of some high land with a large gravel bar circling from its north side around to the south like a giant horseshoe, bounded by a slough on the north and the main channel on the south. Hiram Dodson's lead had extended several hundred feet from near the main river, across the graveled reach, but stopped about 300 feet short of the island. Because this bar was dry in low water, the spot where Koch and Ladzic built their sea wall and lead was covered only when the river was in spate.

19

FIRST PORTABLES

It was commonly believed that a fishwheel could be built or placed at any spot on the river and gulp millions of salmon in about the same way that whales engulf "kril" in the Antarctic seas, but this is not true. Relatively few sites were available where a stationary wheel could capture salmon in profitable numbers. Thousands of dollars were spent futilely, building wheels at positions where no salmon entered the dipways.

It was therefore natural that river men should concentrate on the development of portable wheels. Scow wheels have been mentioned before, but their evolution is interesting. Since double scow-type floating wheels and catamarans existed on the Roanoke and Pee Dee rivers, it may be assumed that the river men developed portable wheels before William Rankin McCord built his floating dipper on the north side of Bradford Island, but no records have been found to support this assumption. From McCord's use of logs as floats to support the rotor of his first catamaran, it is reasonable to believe that the men on the eastern streams also used such supports.

McCord's daughter and his grandson, as well as older river men, confirmed the use of logs as floats supporting the first portable wheel on the Columbia, but no one knew the details. It is likely that the first one, minus any devices to control the elevation of the wheel, was soon altered to give this necessary flexibility of operation. Floats of milled lumber soon followed.

The use of leads as fish diverters became increasingly common at the Cascades, but it was exceed-ingly difficult to fit the two cumbersome wide floats and the dipper assembly of a catamaran into a lead opening, and at the same time prevent the escape of fish. Hence, in the early development of floating or scow wheels it became necessary to invent a system whereby the rotor itself could be supported in such a way that it alone could revolve in a lead opening only slightly wider than the dips.

This was achieved by affixing a long, strong boom to each float so that the two timbers extended downstream beyond the floats. Opposite ends of the rotor axle were attached in bearings to the farther end of each boom; the rotor was thus supported between the projecting timbers and could be lowered into or raised from the openings purposely built into the fishwheel leads. A raised framework or derrick built at the middle of the two floats gave support for tackle to make these adjustments.

From the foregoing design it was easy to evolve to the stronger and less expensive single scow as a support for the twin rear booms and scoop assembly.

For one dollar per cord, the pioneers cut cordwood on the mountain slopes south of Cascade Locks, or north of Stevenson, and hauled it to the river banks where it was loaded onto scows for delivery to The Dalles to be used as fuel. Such scows together with mast for sail were available on the Columbia and were adapted to fishwheel use later.

Hans Lillegard of Stevenson, Washington, was one of many who supplied this cordwood—which was also sold as fuel to the stern- and sidewheelers.

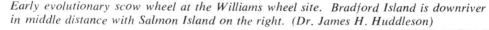

Early evolutionary scow wheel at the Williams wheel site. Bradford Island is downriver in middle distance with Salmon Island on the right. (Dr. James H. Huddleson)

Right: *William Rankin McCord who constructed the third fishwheel on the Columbia. (Aubrey Archer)*

Center: *Scow wheel at the Cascades loaded with blueback salmon, about 1890. (Oregon Historical Society)*

Bottom: *Warren's No. 2 scow. Eric Enquist tended this wheel, 1902-05. One year it captured 80 tons of salmon and blueback. "It was here I caught the largest salmon I ever saw—84 pounds," said Enquist. (Eleanor Rutledge)*

PIONEER MYRON B. KELLY

Prior to 1887, Ira Dodson's neighbor, Myron B. Kelly, built a 50x75-foot pulp mill just west of the mouth of McCord Creek. The main building was two stories high, sheltering five sandstone grindstones in their metal housings and a wood supply. Sheds were built across the ends of the 2-story section. In one lean-to, a water-powered circular saw cut the 4-foot wood sections into shorter lengths to fit into the grinders. The latter were 18 or 24 inches wide by 5 feet in diameter, rotating in strong metal cases against the pulp blocks.

A series of rubber and fabric belts transferred power from the water wheel to various shafts throughout the mill. Other belts, shafts, and wheels delivered power to the grinders, power saw, and additional machinery. When discarded, the belts were used by the scow wheel men to make check valves in the square bilge pumps; hence the mill became a small part of the fishwheel story.

From a point above the second falls, Kelly built a flume northward around the face of the cliff, far above the plant. The 600-foot conduit was connected to a 2,800-foot length of 24-inch steel pipe, which carried water down the mountain to the mill turbine. A small tramway was erected, with 2x4s for rails, on which a 4-wheeled car hauled whatever was needed by the construction and maintenance crews working on the steep slope of the Columbia River Gorge. A hand-cranked windlass located high on the mountainside, at the work site, winched the loaded cart up to the work area.

At one time a Chinese cook served Kelly and his crew. When the men were anchoring the flume to the rock, the Chinaman took their food and utensils to them on the car. After they had eaten, he reloaded his gear and prepared to walk down the precipitous slope, the method of descent he preferred. But the men nagged at him to ride in the cart, which he finally did. However, instead of cranking the chef down, as safe procedure would have indicated, they took a turn around the windlass drum with a manila rope which soon broke, causing the car to run away and jump the track, scattering Chinaman, dishes, pots, and pans over the hillside. Fortunately, the accident did not seriously injure the cook. After hastily descending to his rescue, the men asked about his ride, and in answer he screeched, "Huh, allee same lailload." He never again rode the cart.

Myron B. Kelly's pulp mill dock (far right) and Warren's Cannery, about 1902. Dodson's upper wheel shows at far left with Mosquito Island in center. The scow wheel out from the island (center right) was originally built and owned by Hiram Dodson. Note the long lead on shore of the island. (William Sams, II)

Cottonwood bolts for use in Kelly's pulp mill, which is just out of picture at mouth of McCord Creek. Photo, taken about 1908, shows numerous fishwheels in the vicinity. (Mrs. Ritter)

Bears in the vicinity of the mill caused some minor excitement. While returning along the railroad from the post office at Bonneville to the pulp mill, Nels Halvorsen heard some noise in a swampy salmonberry thicket off to one side. He threw a rock in that direction, and "By Yesus, out yumped a bear." Nels started to run, discarding his coat and hat as he went, with the bear close behind. Fortunately the bruin was discouraged by a short bridge over Rockcrusher Creek. Nels was winded when he reached the mill, but managed to gasp out the reason for his agitation. His associates sallied forth to dispose of the culprit, but found only the hastily discarded hat and coat. Another time, Jim Stradley, also a mill hand, was working up on the mountain when he spotted a bear nearby. He fired his muzzle-loading rifle, but the bruin, only mildly annoyed, merely ambled over to a tree and scratched his back.

Woodcutters were employed to cut cottonwood along both shores of the river and haul it to the pulp-plant landing. A sail-powered wood scow brought the material from across the river. In 1887, Kelly approached an employment agency in Portland for a white-fir woodcutter, and William Sams, Sr., fresh from Minnesota, gained the assignment. Sams wanted to "try out" the West before bringing his family to settle. He was sent out to the mill by train in a snowstorm during January 1888. Temperature was at zero and snow was blowing level from the east and piling into typical Columbia Gorge drifts. With two feet of snow covering the ground, Kelly thought the weather too rough, but Sams had worked in Minnesota logging camps and was accustomed to such conditions. He cut 25 cords of white fir during this winter period, but it proved to be too spongy for use, and when Kelly reverted to cottonwood, Sams transferred to millwork.

After Kelly completed his pulp plant he found there was inadequate water from McCord Creek to power the mill during dry seasons. He then assigned his men the task of diverting Moffett Creek into McCord Creek, entailing dam construction and the excavation of a 200-foot ditch between the two. Moffett Creek water supply begins at a meadow near the west side of Tanner Canyon, a mile south of the point of attempted diversion, and runs over the lava surface on top of the mountain. Its canyon was only 10 to 12 feet deep compared to the Kelly Canyon which was 75 feet. A tree was felled across the Moffett waters to serve as a dam. Upright poles were placed against the horizontal log; brush, twigs, and mud were used to complete the barrier.

Of the results, William "Bill" Sams, II, wrote (January 31, 1964): "A little water began to run through the ditch and started to wash a channel to McCord Creek, but it did not run long enough to cut out across the ridge. The current found an opening at one end of the dam and resumed its original course. When I saw it in 1898 and again in 1908, the large log and some of the short ones were still in place."

The mill had its own version of a kind of "ski lift." A trashrack of 1x4s—placed on edge an inch apart in the forebay high on the mountain—prevented leaves and brush from entering the sluice which regulated the flow of water. During the fall rains, a large amount of trash accumulated on the barrier. To clear this, workmen ascended the mountain on a bosun's chair attached to an aerial tramway. The passenger and pulley were hauled upward from below by a small cable running through a sheave at the upper end of the highline.

About 11 o'clock one night in 1910, trash stopped the water flow, and worker Al Morton was sent up to remove the debris. As he neared the top, the rigging broke, causing him with his kerosene lantern to fall and tumble more than a hundred feet down the mountainside. However, he landed unhurt on a ledge cushioned by snow, stopping just short of the sheer drop. Somehow Morton made his way to the top to complete his mission, even though he had lost the lantern when he fell.

After repeated forest fires had devastated timberlands on the top of the mountain, the water supply diminished to the point where the mill was unprofitable. Besides, all pulp bolts had to be hauled to the mill on scows from downriver, and the pulp hauled back to the paper mills. For these reasons the operation was abandoned. All machinery except the dynamo was removed prior to 1917; after the generator was taken away, the building was used as a workshop by Eric Enquist from March 1920, until the fishwheel era ended. The mill and bunkhouses collapsed in the late 1930s.

For a number of years the concrete slab foundation could be observed from the scenic old Columbia River Highway, but blackberry vines now blanket the area. "Junkies" have salvaged almost all the pipe, though some can yet be found hundreds of feet above the river and old mill site. One of Kelly's grindstones, used to reduce pulp bolts to minute wood fibers, was later used as a weight on his dock to keep it from floating away. When the dock collapsed, the stone fell into the river. Skamania County historians with the aid of scuba divers may locate and recover it some day.

After establishing his pulp mill on the flat land near the western banks of McCord Creek, Kelly, in 1890, decided to claim a few of the salmon surging past his land. He proceeded to build a stationary wheel on the upstream side of the gravel bar deposited by the creek. The structure stood so long that several river men and historians wrongly gave it the honor of being the first such machine on the Columbia. A log crib approximately 20x35 feet and 12 feet high on the shore side of the dipway supported the 35x8-foot, 3-dip wheel. Unlike many similar structures in the Cascades region, this one did not come into possession of Frank Warren, but was retained by Kelly until his death.

Kelly must have built his wheel well because it withstood the savagery of the 1894 flood, which claimed so many other wheels in the Celilo area and the Cascades. High waters did, though, cut a new channel inside the shore lead. Of the wheel as it appeared in early June 1894, William Sams wrote: "I can still see it with the gins above water and the dips raised as high as possible to escape the sullen, muddy waters."

McCord Creek continued to deposit gravel and silt below the lead and dippers to such a degree that it became necessary to abandon the old crib and dipway and rebuild farther out into the river. No crib was included in this later structure. A long incline plane of closely spaced iron bars angling upward was installed in the new dipway to raise the fish to the arc of the dips, but an opening existed below the upstream end of the fish riser, making a trap for driftwood. The innovation was removed after a season or more of use.

Both new and old wheels were profitable "but were not gold mines." Chinooks and bluebacks were commonly taken plus some carp, shad, suckers, squawfish, Dolly Varden trout, lampreys, and sea-run cutthroats.

The Kelly Wheel was another which caught numerous large sturgeon. One morning while temporarily tending the wheel, Sams found a large quantity of sturgeon roe strewn about the fishhouse and on adjacent decking. A large female had entered the discharge chute or opening from one of the dips, tail first, and its body had been cut in two between the rotor and gins, the severed head portion falling back into the river. Twelve quarts of prime caviar eggs were scooped up, but gallons more must have been lost through the numerous cracks between decking members. The large sturgeon captured were usually too long to exit rapidly through the discharge chute, and thus were mutilated by movement of the dipper assembly past the rotor elevating gins.

24

Andrew Vanstrom and 673-pound female white sturgeon taken in McGowan fishwheel, 1912. Note large fishwheel beams, bullwheel, and trap door to fish room. (Al Hendricks)

HAMILTON'S SCOW

Off the Washington shore a large island (Hamilton) was formed about one mile below the later site of Bonneville Dam, where the river deposited detritus from Cascade Slide. In pioneer days, S. M. Hamilton was granted possession of the island through a donation land claim, and he and his family farmed the area for decades. Early aviators found refuge on the island's sandy landing strips.

A high-water channel, Hamilton Slough, separates this island from the Washington mainland. A few hundred feet below the mouth of Hamilton Creek, on the north bank of the slough, Hamilton's son Bill attached the landward portion of a medium-sized scow wheel to a sizable rock which served both as anchor and inside shunt. A short 30-foot vertical pole (picket) outboard lead extended diagonally downstream. A few individual fish of other species may have entered the dips of Hamilton's Wheel, but the catch was almost entirely blueback, and the wheel worked only at high water. In the memory of the old-timers, there were years when not enough water poured downstream to operate the wheel, but it did well when the water rose to an adequate level.

Both site and scow wheel were soon abandoned.

View of Gorge in 1903 showing (1) Bill Hamilton's blueback wheel, (2) Hamilton Wheel on Hamilton Island, (3) scow wheel lead owned by Jason Hamilton, (4) Sams' Wheel No. 2 on upper end of Ives Island, (5) Moffett Creek Wheel, (6) Wheel No. 20, (7) Hamilton Island Slough, (8) Greenleaf Slough, and (9) Hamilton Creek. (Kiser Bros.)

CASTLE ROCK WHEEL

Downriver from the Hamilton Scow was the Castle Rock Stationary Wheel. Although Lewis and Clark gave the name Beacon Rock to the large volcanic plug situated on the Washington shore 5 miles below Bonneville Dam, local residents somehow came to call it "Castle Rock," and that became the name of the wheel located there.

Jack Erickson, whom Sams and Enquist remember as a strong, affable Swede, originally built the Castle Rock dipper in 1896, on the north side of Pierce (Mosquito) Island. The wheel's outward lead, of horizontal-bar type, was about 150 feet long, with an inboard fence of 100 feet. Driven piling formed the main anchor for the wheel and log cribbing. In this case the crib was made of driven piling, but was not filled with rocks. However, in about a year, silt settled around the lead and the structure became a "white elephant."

Joseph Paquet, Portland shipbuilder and angler, in whose pockets "money did jingle," had arrived on the scene about 1894-95 and installed a scow wheel on the south side of Ives Island. Desiring to increase his fortune with fishwheels, Paquet asked Erickson if he were willing to sell. With carefully feigned reluctance, Erickson haggled and finally agreed to part with his "white elephant" for $1,800. The two men then separated and while Paquet examined his original installation on Ives Island, Erickson hastily took the next train to Portland, where he awaited Paquet's arrival to complete the deal.

The new owner soon learned the worthlessness of the wheel, whereupon he cut off the piling (1898) at gravel level and moved the entire assembly to Bill Hamilton's beach on the Washington mainland at the western end of Hamilton Slough, half a mile east of Beacon Rock and opposite the lower end of Ives Island. While at the Hamilton site, the wheel functioned in high water to take a moderate catch of blueback (primarily), spring chinooks, and steelhead.

Icehouse stationary fishwheel and remnant of Erickson Wheel on near shore, middle distance. Postcard from which picture was copied bore postmark, December 25, 1908. (Mrs. Thomas Binford)

Banks on Columbia River, Oregon.

Icehouse Wheel at low water. (John Butler)

Apparently Paquet entered into some kind of partnership with the McGowan Packing Company and also with Bill Hamilton; Hamilton owned the land, and Paquet and McGowan became fishing partners. In 1917, Martin Enquist bought the Paquet interest and became partners with McGowan. After Enquist's death, his son, Eric, inherited and superintended operations of the Castle Rock Wheel until wheels were prohibited.

Admirers of Beacon Rock today have the Spokane, Portland & Seattle Railway in part to thank for its existence. In an effort to block expansion of James J. Hill's Columbia River Gorge S. P. & S., Edward Harriman, Director of the Union Pacific and the Southern Pacific, began an apparent renovation of the early Cascade Portage Railway between Cascade Rapids and Hamilton Island. Following a hotly contested court trial, S. P. & S. won, and by right of eminent domain claimed a strip of land including a deposit of red soil near Beacon Rock. However, the dispossessed owner of the strip, Turner Leavens, considered the strip of land far more valuable than the offered payment.

Already angered by a railroad development which once before had caused him to leave the Cascade Locks area, he employed every stratagem possible to stop progress of the S. P. & S., finally taking the case to court. The reddish soil of several shades, which Leavens claimed to be a paint mine, was a type of soapstone or clay located along the river bank. He lost his suit when S. P. & S. lawyers exhibited two containers at the trial—one of ground brick, the other soil from Leavens' "mine" mixed like paint—and proved there was no apparent difference. Earlier, Leavens had planned to blow Beacon Rock to pieces to obtain jetty material, and already had drilled "coyote" (powder) holes deep into its mass at the southern side, but when the railroad won the litigation, Beacon Rock was saved.

According to Bill Sams, Turner Leavens' quarry scheme had been another plot to stop the railroad. But despite such obstacles and the powerful forces of Edward Harriman, James Hill's north bank railroad was completed in 1908, to compete with the rails on the south bank—and provide more than ample transportation for the regions served.

THE IRON WHEEL

Four successive wheels rose at Moffett Creek, across from Hamilton Island, on the Oregon side, and all were locally known by the same name of Iron or Moffett Creek Wheel. Tom Moffett, one of the early settlers, homesteaded his place before the railroad came and improved his holdings by clearing it of trees and brush before planting an orchard. The claim extended up the side of the Gorge and could have been 160 acres under the Homestead Act, or a donation land claim. Moffett, on whose land the wheels were erected, probably had some interest in the wheels, at least in the beginning.

According to Bill Sams: "Tom Moffett was a real old-timer in these parts because he was in possession of the Oregon property before the railroad was built, the latter having only a narrow 60-foot right-of-way through his land. . . . At some time Moffett must have lived on the Oregon place, for while I never did see any signs of a house, there was an orchard and blackberries, red raspberries, rose bushes, and also strawberries gone wild. When we came in 1889 he was not living here, so I think he started with his hot springs resort on the Washington shore sometime in the 1880s."

The first Moffett Wheel was among the earliest wheels on the river. In late 1882 L. J. MacLeod, a carpenter, paid a $500 fee to William Rankin McCord & Associates to build a wheel near Moffett Creek. Made mostly of iron, it became known as the Iron Wheel. Nevertheless, it was a flimsy, ramshackle affair and soon gave out.

Moffett Wheel No. 2, which replaced it, was constructed of wood with the familiar spiral, McCord-type dips. While it was in operation, the pile of rusty iron pipe and remnants of the first machine moldered on the adjacent bank. In 1893, Frank Warren gained possession of the wheel as payment for a loan. Warren came into ownership of many of his wheels when the original owners chose to tender their machines to reduce, or pay, their debts.

The 1894 flood ripped No. 2 entirely away, but early the following year, Warren erected a third wheel at the Moffett Creek site. It was operating there in 1902 when Eric Enquist arrived on the scene. Its dippers caught a great variety of fish in all sizes but not many sturgeon. Joel Westerlund said the Moffett Creek Wheel was the most profitable one that Warren owned. Some of Warren's

Rebuilt Iron or Moffett Creek Wheel is in foreground, with Sams' No. 2 across channel on Ives Island bar. Castle Rock Wheel shows on Washington shore nearer Beacon Rock. Another wheel lead can be seen faintly on the south side of Ives Island. (University of Oregon Library)

wheels, like Thornton Williams', caught many fish but repairs and overhead proved excessive.

Rebuilt of wood by Warren in 1910, the Iron Wheel functioned until all such wheels were outlawed. Thereafter, by substituting a box-like enclosure where the dippers had once turned, Warren converted the structure into a fish trap . . . but very few fish were captured. Warren Packing Company's daily wheel-catch records indicate that a number of wheels, including the Williams and McCord dippers, were converted to such traps with the outlawing of wheels—and with equally poor success.

Gradual attrition wore the fourth Moffett Creek structure away, piece by piece, and the remainder disappeared in the 1930 high water.

Prior to construction of the Iron Wheel, and before William Sams, Sr., arrived in the Columbia Gorge area in 1887, Thomas Moffett built a conventional Columbia River twin-boom scow wheel at the upper end of a small eddy approximately 200 feet downstream from the Rudolph Snow Scow

Wheel. This was attached to a very steep rocky bank on the Oregon shore between Tanner and Moffett creeks. The short 60-foot, 2-dipway lead was made of vertical poles set 3 inches apart. The wheel was a "small, dinky" 3-dip affair sweeping only about 9 feet deep, but it caught some "whopping" big salmon. Of this structure, young Bill Sams wrote, "I never saw this wheel in operation, but did see the lead that remained, and I heard Dad tell about the big salmon it took in the spiral, McCord-type dips."

Because the wheel could be used only during high water, it was a blueback and chinook wheel. True to his thrifty nature, Moffett floated his fish down to the cannery in barrel floats to avoid payment of railroad freight. Although the fish captured were large, apparently too few were taken because the site was abandoned between 1887 and 1890. The scow may have been sold and moved to a more productive site, but ravages of time and succeeding spring freshets finally obliterated the remnants of the lead about 1905.

Closer view of the rebuilt Moffett Creek Wheel. (Oregon Historical Society)

Sternwheeler Hattie Bell *approaching Moffett's Landing about 1890. The locomotive was used to haul fish from Warren's wheels to this landing where they were picked up and taken to the cannery. After the flood of 1894 Warren built a personal railroad from here to wheels 3 and 20. Wheel 3 is shown over the top of the post on the river bank. Note the fish boxes on the beach. (George B. Abdill)*

Moffett's Hot Springs. (Wid Senter)

Tanner Creek Scow Wheel looking toward Washington shore and Table Mountain.
(University of Oregon Library)

Warren's Scow 2 in foreground, and the McCord Wheel on Bradford Island across the
slough, 1910. (Eric Enquist)

TANNER CREEK WHEEL

Picture postcards were made of a number of salmon wheels on the river, and Scow No. 4, the Tanner Creek Wheel, was a popular subject—not only because of its graceful lines but also because of its accessibility. Stored in the Oregon Room of the University of Oregon Library is a wonderfully sharp and well-preserved photographic plate of this wheel by George M. Weister, the famous pioneer photographer.

Neither the builder nor the date of what became Warren's Scow No. 4 is known, but Warren came into possession of it, probably in payment of a loan, in the late 1880s or early 1890s, about the same time he took over the Tom Moffett Wheel at the mouth of Moffett Creek. Scow 4 was situated at the mouth of Tanner Creek and at the west end of Colonel Joseph S. Ruckel's Oregon Portage Railway, which was used earlier in competition with the Cascades Portage on the Washington shore. The builders may have had to rip out some of the old Oregon Portage Railway incline to drive piling for Scow 4. The Tanner Creek, and also the Moffett Creek fishwheels, were really pioneers, next in line with the McCord and Williams wheels.

The timbered area between the river and the high bank near the Tanner Creek Wheel was a mecca for picnickers who came up on Sundays to watch the scoops dip fish from the river. The sylvan setting here was probably one of the most romantic spots in the Gorge. The easy slope to the river, large fir trees in the background, and the excellent view up and down the river made the area a popular trysting place. Poachers also found this fishwheel a profitable place to visit. The rotor was untended a large portion of the time, and anyone could crawl out there to get a fish.

In 1907, Joel Westerlund repaired and improved the lead and installed a new scow. Although this wheel took some blueback, it was not a profitable endeavor and probably terminated about 1910. In 1959, Lawrence Stevens wrote from Oak Grove, Oregon, that he and his father had tended this wheel around 1902. He described how the fish were transported to Warren's Cannery, attached to barrel or cask floats.

Tanner Creek Scow Wheel lead is in foreground. Oregon Portage Railway western terminus piling shows just above fishwheel lead. Wheel 20 can be seen across the river, and Wheel 3 upstream from it. (Dorothy P. Nile)

Oregon's first railway, the Oregon Portage Railroad, entirely of wood except for iron strap on the wooden rails, was built in 1858-59 to compete with a similar line on the Washington side. It extended from Bonneville to Cascade Locks, and took in all riverside lands including the present Bonneville picnic grounds. The Union Pacific today traverses almost the exact alignment.

Colonel Joseph Ruckel's Oregon Portage Railroad before the Oregon Pony came to the Cascades. Note the strap iron facing on the 6"x6" timber rails. (Frank N. Parker)

Left: *Residence of Joseph Bailey—superintendent of Oregon Portage Railroad—at the mouth of Eagle Creek. Looking down Bradford Slough, note mule pulling a flat car across portage railroad trestle.* Right: *The Middle Landing of the railroad showing trestle and what must be a warehouse. Colonel Joseph Ruckel settled here in 1855. (Marjorie Shantz)*

Colonel Joseph Ruckel's water-powered sawmill and flume at the mouth of Eagle Creek, 1867. William Sams, II, recalled seeing pile of slash prior to the 1894 flood, which erased all trace of the mill and slash pile. (George B. Abdill)

One of Frank Warren's casks and a harness for floating fish to his cannery. The long skewer or needle was used to thread a line through the eyes and head of salmon so that they could be secured to the two loops of rope below the cask. (William Sams, II)

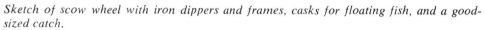

Sketch of scow wheel with iron dippers and frames, casks for floating fish, and a good-sized catch.

SHIPMENTS BY CASK

During the period in which fishwheels were developed, when vast numbers of salmon yet ran in the river, neither the gasoline trucks nor power boats were common to carry the fish from some wheels in the Cascades Rapids region to the cannery at Warrendale. Later, Warren had a succession of steam launches but the earlier ones were inadequately powered and had difficulty breasting the excessive river velocities at the Upper Cascades. Not until the completion of Cascade Locks in 1896—well after the day when the salmon resource was "inexhaustible" — could river craft bypass these rapids; and since the wagon roads through the gorge were little better than trails—well nigh impassable during the rainy season—it was a real problem to transport fish to the cannery.

Though there was a passable wagon road between Cascade Locks and Eagle Creek as early as 1856, evidently neither the Warren nor McGowan packing companies used it. This would indicate that, prior to the completion of rails along the south bank of the river — by the Oregon Railway & Navigation Company in 1882—no land transportation existed to move fish from the Oregon wheels to the Warrendale Cannery. Instead, the catch of the Oregon wheels above Warrendale was floated downstream toward the cannery by means of wooden casks or barrels. No one knows who originated this means of shipping fish; however, by the time the railroad

was completed, this float method had proved less expensive and much easier and faster than shipment by rail or by wagon on the Oregon side of the river.

On the Washington side, many casks tangled with—or were hung up and lost in—brush and eddies, so the barrel system was abandoned. After that, the Cascade Portage Railroad and Warren's special fish railroad and boats were used to move fish from wheels on the Washington side. Conditions were bad on both sides of the river when an east wind blew.

Bill Sams gives the following first-hand account of floating casks down to Warren's Cannery, below McCord Creek: "A strand from quarter-inch manila rope, cut in correct lengths for the different groups, was passed through the head and both eyes of each fish by means of a long needle. Then the ends of the cord were tied together with a square knot. A rope about 8 feet long was permanently fastened to the barrel at each end, upon which the various strings of fish were secured until there were enough to make up a load. Eight bluebacks, six steelhead, four medium chinooks (up to 20 pounds in size), and two large chinooks—or one extra-large chinook—were attached to each string. Several or many such strings were attached to each float. The weight was governed by the need to lift the fish over the gunwale of the pickup boat.

Nerka II, about 1906, famous steam-powered fish pick-up boat at Moffett's Landing. William Sams is at the bow with line. This craft transported salmon from the Cascades wheels downstream to the Warrendale Cannery.

"If enough fish were available, each barrel or cask carried only one species. Sturgeon float barrels were painted red for easy identification. Salmon pickup men would let these drift by, to be retrieved farther downstream by sturgeon fishermen at Oneonta.

"When 800 to 1,500 pounds—or the buoyancy of the barrel—had been reached, the loose ends of the 8-foot lines were tied to the barrel lashings of the cask. These casks would support a much greater weight of fish than their volume would indicate because the fish were buoyed by the water.

"Each cask had a harness with a loop on the top for grasping, plus the two ropes leading from the bottom ends of the float upon which the bunches of fish were hung. A linen tag bearing the fishwheel number, date, and pounds of each species was attached to that portion of the rope harness stretched across the top of the barrel. Thus equipped, the entire assemblage was ready to start its trip to the cannery. A wet slideway was usually provided down which the cask and fish were lowered into the river.

"At the cannery a watchman, equipped with field glasses and stationed in a lookout balcony, sighted the casks and notified a boatman who went out and lifted the float and fish into his boat. Coded blasts

of a steam whistle guided the pickup boatman to the drifting fish."

Warren's men constructed Scow 2 about 1896. The lead of this wheel had three dipways for successive scoop positions as the river level changed, and a snail-shell dipper rotated during high water close to the Oregon shore. A productive enterprise, it remained in use till the end of the fishwheel era.

Occasionally some of the fish barrels would become trapped a few hundred feet below Scow 2 in Derrick Eddy, especially when an east wind was howling down the Gorge. To retrieve the fish and casks it was necessary for one or two men to row into the dangerous waters and tow the unit out to the main current.

Several years prior to 1902, Warren's men grew tired of the hazardous boat work involved in removing the trapped barrels from the eddy below Scow 2 and erected a derrick pole with swinging boom on the point above China Eddy for use in grappling for and casting the fish casks free from the whirlpool. The men working on shore used pike poles or weighted hooks on throwing-lines to pull floats and fish from the water. The casks were then fixed to the end of the flat, swinging boom and swung outward by means of lines into the river, where sufficient cur-

Warren's Scow 2 on Oregon shore opposite Bradford Island about 1894. The mast and sail rigging indicates that this scow formerly sailed wood to The Dalles. Note the metal dipper frames. (Oregon Historical Society)

Warren's Scow Wheel No. 2 on Oregon shore opposite Bradford Island. Note the openings in the lead to accommodate the scow wheel during various stages of high water. Derrick on the river bank below wheel lead was used to retrieve cask floats and fish from the eddy, and send them on downstream to the cannery. (Dorothy P. Nile)

rent would whisk them to the cannery. Eric Enquist had this to say about Derrick Eddy:

"One time when I was working to catch a mean fish barrel in Derrick Eddy, a naked dead man drifted in also. He had been a deck hand on *The Dalles City* steamer. One other morning as I was sweating there in the eddy, Joel Westerlund came out on the McCord Wheel and started shouting and pointing toward my cabin near Scow 2. Two strangers had climbed in through the window. After their arrest I had to go to Portland as a witness against them. Strict company man that he was, Joel Westerlund then docked me a day's wages for the time spent at the trial. At an earlier time, he had deducted half a day's pay when I took off a half hour to kill a swan. In addition, he also ate half the bird!"

Although it was a risky procedure, Enquist and Westerlund on occasion would be compelled to take a skiff into other dangerous stretches of water, lift the barrel into the boat with fish trailing behind, and pull out into the current to release the cask where it could float on downstream. This was hard work before gasoline engine days. As Al Hendricks commented, "At low flows, the water racing down through Bradford Slough was 'rougher than hell.'"

There was no problem at China Eddy where the waters created a circular current below a projection of the shoreline lava-outcropping now known to geologists as Bonney (Bonneville) Rock. The dam's navigation locks obliterated both the China and Derrick eddies.

One day following the peak of the spring flood, Al Hendricks had become so engrossed in his task of guiding barrels and fish from the Williams Wheel down into Bradford Channel that he forgot to watch his drift. When he became aware of his surroundings, he was being swept inexorably into the wild water between Bradford Island and the Oregon mainland. He abandoned his fish in desperation, leaped to furl and stow the sail, grabbed oars, and in the wildest and most terrifying ride of his career, guided the craft through the maelstrom to safety below, his boat by this time half full of water. "I didn't know I was so strong," he later recalled.

Every year a number of barrels were lost, but a barrel with 700 or 800 pounds of fish did not mean so much in those days when 24 to 30 barrels a day were released from four wheels. However, should a floating cask drift past the cannery, Warren would

pay a reward of five dollars to anyone returning it with the attached load of fish. . . . It was also not uncommon for fish pirates to waylay these loaded floating barrels and remove the fish.

Enquist voted the Williams Wheel the best in the region. The catch was steady. The McCord Wheel (later known as the Harrison or B-1) was good but did not equal the Williams. In 1902, at the Williams Wheel, Eric (who rose at dawn each day) floated 3 tons of fish downstream by 7 a.m. The fish were strung and attached to casks as described, and when the cannery called on the newly installed telephone with instructions, usually about 6 a.m., these casks were started on their way. After lunch, about 1 p.m., the second shipment was set afloat. Fish caught after 3 p.m. would be held until the next morning.

Reconstructed Williams fishwheel immediately prior to the flood of 1894, which removed wheel and houses. (University of Oregon Library)

Warren's Cannery at Warrendale, Oregon, showing some of the cannery crew.
(William Sams, II)

On one Fourth of July, about 1912, the Warren Cannery crew had planned to finish canning the day's accumulation of salmon by noon to gain a free half day, but on this particular holiday occurred one of the greatest runs of bluebacks known to the river. The crew was required to can an additional shipment; and to make matters worse, one cask carrying approximately half a ton of fish hung up on the outside lead of the Snow-Totten Wheel, while still another was caught on the inside lead. This caused Bill Sams both exasperating labor and danger in freeing them, for his job was to retrieve casks from the river. Bill was able to release the one on the outside after moderate effort, but he encountered difficulty with the float on the inside lead. The skipper nosed the *Nerka* in from downstream, and Bill, by climbing up over the horizontal bars, was able to work the shipment of fish over the fence and into the boat. By the time he had accomplished this, his Independence Day celebration was ruined.

Warren's B-7 was a scow dipper installed about 1917 adjacent to the large rocks in midstream northeast of Bradford Island. The revolving dipnet was moved to this location when the Tanner Creek site was abandoned. In giving numbers to his salmon dippers, Warren prefixed the initial "B" to indicate those adjacent to Bradford Island. Salmon Island (Boat Rock) as well as other rocks jutting out of the water close above the Warren construction headquarters on Bradford Island were somehow considered a portion of this bit of land.

Among the numerous fishwheels supplying the Warren Cannery was the Lynn Wheel. Not one of the dozens of people interviewed for this book knew Mr. Lynn's first name, nor when in the very early wheel era he built his salmon scoop, but it is generally agreed he placed it a few hundred feet too far downstream, on the northwest shore of Bradford

Island, where very few fish passed. It was anchored opposite Warren's stationary No. 3, located on the Washington shore. Warren may have loaned money to the builder, and when the debt was not paid, assumed ownership of the wheel. At any rate, Warren came into possession of the Lynn Wheel.

This wheel is recalled as a 32-foot-diameter, 3-dip machine. Eric Enquist saw it turning in 1902, although not many fish were being caught. An inshore 40- to 50-foot horizontal bar lead extended from Bradford Island out to the rock-filled crib. The outer fence, which was approximately 150 feet in length, stretched downstream toward the Washington shore. Both Sams and Enquist have related how Warren's men would lower the dips of this island wheel to start it running, then go away and leave it untended. The meager catch was checked at daily intervals. Any fish caught were trundled by cart or wheelbarrow to the McCord site, then floated downstream to the cannery. By 1905 the piling had been sawed off at water surface and the crib reduced to a few pile stumps and rocks, some of which could still be seen in 1960, when tailwater below the dam dropped to a very low level.

Because communication played such an important part in the timing of fishwheel "shipments" by cask, a few words about installation of telephones seem in order. Warren installed telephones about 1896 or 1897 to connect his cannery, the Bradford Island office, and each of his Oregon wheels; his Washington wheels were not so equipped. The line from the Oregon shore to the island was strung between two sizable fir trees. Glass insulators similar to those of the railroad company were used to insulate the lines. When trees fell upon his original wires, Warren arranged to attach his telephone line to the railroad telegraph poles. His wheel sites on the Oregon shore were also leased from the railroad.

Scow B-7 (with tender's shack at rocks in middle of river) and Wheel B-18 at lower end of Salmon Island. Government Slide shows clearly across the river. (Dorothy P. Nile)

Beginning of construction of the upper Bonneville Dam cofferdam in 1933. Wheel B-18 shows at downstream end of Salmon Island. The Williams fishwheel appears on the Oregon shore beyond B-18. (Fern McGee)

EARLY SCOWS

In 1887 or earlier, McCord had located the first Columbia River scow wheel—a catamaran—on the north side of Bradford Island about 500 feet downstream from the present southern end of the Bonneville Dam spillway. Its rotor was supported by and dipped between large logs. Shortly after its construction, Warren gained possession and it became his B-3 Scow. He maintained a succession of rotifers and leads at this spot until all wheels were outlawed in Oregon—though it was about a year more before the ban was enforced. Bradford Island, named for the pioneer steamboat and Portage Railway operators, Daniel and Putnam Bradford, is a part of Oregon's Multnomah County.

Warren's Swedes soon perceived the inability of a catamaran and rotor to fit into a gap in any type of fish lead, and thereafter substituted the classical twin-boom scow with rotor fitting into an opening in a horizontal bar lead, thereby increasing the efficiency of this location. Bill Sams said, "In addition to the advantage of fitting a narrow rotor into a hole of the same size, the reason Warren didn't continue to use catamaran scows was because they were not strong enough. A one-piece wide scow could be braced better and was more rigid than two narrow pontoons fastened together on top only. When a steamboat went by, the catamaran Dad owned would wiggle like a snake."

Scow B-3, replacing the double-float rig, had curved crooks or dipper arms similar to those patented by McCord, which were adopted by Warren. Leads observed in 1890 were of the horizontal-bar type, the inside one being 40 to 50 feet long while the outside lead, angling downstream, was possibly 60 feet in length.

The long life of this wheel attested to a profitable location, but when compared with high-production wheels of those days it was rated only "fair" by the men who remember it. All species of salmon were caught from the wild waters of the Lower Cascades; however, blueback were not predominant in the catch. Almost all its catch was transported by casks or barrels down to the Warrendale Cannery, except when only a few fish were caught—under 150 pounds—in which case, they were trundled southward across the island to Warren B-1 and there attached to the casks, along with fish from the B-1.

This is thought to be Scow 3 by Warren, on Washington shore above Wheel 15.
(Oregon Historical Society)

Upriver from Bradford Island—the site of the two McCord machines—was the site of the famous old Williams Wheel on the north bank. Later stationary wheels constructed at this location never changed names from the time of the first one in 1879.

After purchasing the flimsy wheel from Williams, about 1884, Warren reconstructed it and extended a lead curving downstream to a great rock which rested about 300 feet out in the channel. Warren scow wheel No. 1, a twin rear-boom type located on the river side of the large rock, was fastened sideways to "lay" posts anchored in the rock and had a cable from the scow upstream to another large rock to hold the scow against the current.

Warren paid $600 a year to the tender of the scow and stationary, a wage considered good for those days. This was in the early 1890s and the tender was William Sams, Sr., who was to keep the wheel in good operating condition and burn any driftwood which collected on the lead. His son, Bill, told of one incident during the burning of trash that proved almost disastrous:

"After the river fell and the trash dried enough to burn, Dad would begin the cleanup by starting a fire some distance from the lead during a west wind so that sparks would be carried away from the installation. This particular time he had been burning the day before, but because the east wind had come up, decided not to start a fire anew. About one o'clock in the afternoon we went to the dam on Ruckel Creek, where the pipeline started, and remained for a time. I happened to look around and saw smoke rolling up, which brought us hurrying back. There was a sprinkler system in the fish house to which water was piped out to the wheel, and by connecting a hose to the pipeline we were able to wet down the side of the crib facing the fire. We saved the wheel, but much of the lead was consumed. This hose was used to wash down the floor in the fish house and served also to keep the fish wet—before we learned that too much water caused the fish to deteriorate. Needless to say, we watched our trash-burning more carefully after that."

The scow, of regular size, was washed away in the 1894 flood, together with both the stationary and lead located on the south side. Because the massive anchor rock had disappeared during the flood, Scow No. 1 was not replaced. Wheel men believe the later stationary wheel was placed farther out toward the channel after the high water.

While en route from the Williams Wheel to Cascade Locks in 1890, Bill Sams and his father came upon the smallest salmon wheel they had seen on the Columbia. A short distance east of Ruckel Creek, which was the eastern boundary of the land leased by the Warren Packing Company from the railroad, the rusty 2-inch pipe axle of this minimal dipper spanned a narrow channel of water between the shore and a mass of rocks 5 or 6 feet out in the river.

Three scoops, possibly 3 feet wide, dipping no more than 2½ or 3 feet, lifted blueback salmon from the shallow channel to a point above the shaft, from which they slid out a wet-board chute into an ordinary fishbox. The latter rested on the rocks beside the chicken-wire-covered dips. A rough cross of 4x6s and rocks supported the axle and gave elevation adjustment to this light, portable wheel, which caught bluebacks exclusively. "A big chinook would have torn this wheel to pieces."

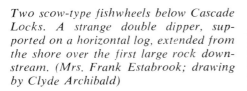

Two scow-type fishwheels below Cascade Locks. A strange double dipper, supported on a horizontal log, extended from the shore over the first large rock downstream. (Mrs. Frank Estabrook; drawing by Clyde Archibald)

48

WILLIAM SAMS

William Sams, Sr., who became one of the early fishwheel operators on the Columbia, got his first real experience in the business when, in 1890, he began operating the Thornton Williams Wheel for Frank Warren. He had become interested in the wheels while homesteading a 39-acre plot he had taken in 1888 when working for Myron Kelly. The homestead bordered the river at the rock-crusher site about two miles west of Bonneville. Shortly thereafter Sams purchased an additional narrow strip of 10 acres between the river and the railroad track. This, with the homestead, gave him approximately 1,000 feet of river frontage. The following year, 1891, he returned to Minnesota for his wife and two children, William (Bill) 4, and Grace, 2. It was shortly after his return to the homestead that he was hired as operator at the Thornton Williams Wheel.

In the family's move to the new location, food and household goods were transported by the steamer *Sakana* to the Bradford Island Landing on the south shore below the McCord Wheel, then loaded on a "stone boat" (sled) pulled by oxen. En route, the animals became frightened and ran away, strewing Mrs. Sams' canned fruit, furniture, and utensils into the brush along the roadway. After the team was calmed, the unbroken pieces were reassembled and hauled to the boat landing at the upper end of the island. From this point, the family, the much-abused wares, and bedding burned from the *Sakana's* boiler sparks were crowded into a sailboat and taken half a mile east to the Williams Wheel site, thus completing a troublesome journey.

They moved back to the homestead near Bonneville the following year, where Sams finally entered the fishwheel industry independently. He invited Ed Nieman to go into partnership with him. He had known Nieman earlier while working at the Williams Wheel, which was then operated by Warren. By this time Nieman had won an enviable reputation as an expert in fishwheel construction. He readily agreed to join Sams. It may seem puzzling that the Warren Company permitted its employees to compete in the industry by erecting a wheel near their own machine, but there were periods when Warren did not have enough work for the entire crew, and the men were forced to seek a livelihood as best they could.

Their first wheel was an unusual 3-dipper catamaran purchased from a man by the name of Higgens. Although it was a catamaran, the rotor was supported on twin rear booms. Two uprights, one on each side, capped by a strong crosspiece, served to support the projecting timbers and dipper assembly with strong chains and cables. Chain blocks strained to raise and lower the rotor—an arduous task. The booms, extending out over the downstream edge of the buoyancy chambers, were hinged at the base of the two guyed gins; but as stated before, a portion of the dips revolved between the two floats. Sturdy cross members, together with the family cabin located upstream from the sweep of the dips, held the parallel barges together. Such strange construction may indicate alteration by Higgens from a conventional catamaran with scoops dipping amidships, to make space for the 14x18-foot cabin, as well as to locate the wheel so that at least part of it would rotate in a lead opening.

The first spring freshet tore the outer lead away. Thereafter, Sams purchased his partner's share and rebuilt the wheel, continuing to use the leaky scow dipper for several years with no modification. By dint of constant and irksome pumping with the old square bilge pumps, he managed to keep the rickety and troublesome craft afloat but was not successful as it dipped only nine or ten feet deep, missing many fish. One fall, however, before being discarded, it captured a surprising number of steelhead. For a period of several days it took about 300 pounds per day. Reluctantly the Warrendale Cannery would accept these fish at a price of 1 to 1½ cents per pound. But Captain Perk Hosford, skipper of the sternwheeler *Ione*, found a market for them in Portland for one cent per pound more than the cannery paid. Myron Kelly, who had been selling his fish secretly at the same place, became quite angry with Sams for "horning in" on his limited outlet.

The *Ione* made daily trips to Warrendale, where she tied up overnight, leaving early in the mornings for Portland. Young Sams had to row the load of steelhead in the evenings to Warrendale, a half mile downstream from his wheel. Usually the wind died down at this time of day, making it impossible to sail home, nor could he row upstream around the Kelly Wheel lead against the exceedingly swift cur-

Sternwheeler Regulator *near Beacon Rock—not Castle Rock, although at one period old-timers called the volcanic plug "Castle Rock." (Oregon Historical Society)*

rent bearing onto the Oregon shore. Hence he was compelled to walk home, then return in the morning for the sailboat. These steelhead of exceptionally large size soon passed, and the opportunity ended.

In the fall of 1898, with funds borrowed from Patrick J. McGowan, Sams built a stationary wheel under the overhanging Eagle Creek formation near the crusher site. The new wheel, Stationary No. 1—considered to be the largest in the Cascades region—was 44 feet in diameter by 8 feet in width. It therefore dipped to about 21 feet, but the water here was almost 90 feet deep, and as before, the majority of the salmon escaped the dips. To close this opening, Sams dumped innumerable cubic yards of talus from the crusher slope into the dipway. He also attempted to lower a large rectangular rock-filled box in the wheelway, but the unit jammed between the piling instead of settling to the bottom. However, it did not interfere with the sweep of the rotor.

In construction of the lead, two parallel lines of 8 to 10 piling were driven 6 feet apart into the river bottom. Then a horizontal timber was bolted to the upper row and the tops of the lower were pulled upstream against the swift current to brace the entire assembly, which shook and swayed alarmingly. Attempts to drive piling into the hard, rocky bottom through 90 feet of rapidly moving water were most difficult, but piledriver Tommy Davidson —an "ingenious damn Yankee"—managed to force

the ends of the slender tree trunks deep enough to last longer than the period of Sams' ownership. The outboard lead extended approximately 70 feet outward toward the middle of the river.

Originally there was no need to erect a shelter on Stationary No. 1, because it was only 300 feet from the family residence, and entirely visible. A walkway from the top of the lead to the bank gave easy access. On its completion, Sams retired the old catamaran, mooring it along the beach a short distance below. Here its cabin served as home to Captain Sherman Brunson Ives for several years until Sams erected a house for the Captain on the island bearing his name—Ives Island. Sams later leased property from Ives with option for renewal. Stationary No. 1 did not take a vast poundage of fish, yet it did pay for itself and did give Sams a minor profit as well. It caught more chinooks than any other species, but took some of all kinds, including many large sturgeon.

Sams' enterprises were beset with troubles. He had borrowed $2,500 from Patrick McGowan, on the basis of a 5-year contract, to build his wheel—which proved highly beneficial to McGowan, not Sams. The agreement was for Sams to deliver all his salmon to the McGowan Cannery at 4 cents per pound, but though the price of salmon rose to 5 cents within two years, McGowan paid Sams no extra compensation.

Before completion of the wheel, trouble with the railroad had occurred. Sams' little tramway, which he planned to use for hauling rock to the wheel dipway, passed under the transcontinental railroad bridge to the river. The railroad replaced this trestle with an earth fill for almost its entire length, necessitating relocation of the tramway to a higher location.

When Sams' plans to build had become known, but prior to actual construction of the wheel, the adjacent upstream landowner, Tom Moffett—with aid and encouragement from Warren—attempted to build a "wood dock" 35 feet below the top of the bank, and only 8 feet above low-water mark, ostensibly for selling wood to passing steamers. In reality, he was trying to prevent access of a piledriver to Sams' wheel niche. Although it was low-water season, this steam-driver outfit had difficulty in punching the piling for the wood dock into the hard, remote bottom of the river, and many poles bounced back to drift away. Only eight or ten remained in the very deep water until they could be fastened together with cross timbers. As a result, the dock was never completed, though a few piling remained.

Tommy Davidson made good use of these few stable uprights to secure his rig while he drove the dipway and lead for Sams. The "wood dock" caused no damage to the Sams establishment until a spring spate loosened some of the long poles. One of these rammed into the wheel dipway, and as the dip came down on top of the pole, several crosspieces were broken before his wheel could be stopped. Only by laboriously raising the rotor in its gins was the log freed to float downstream. The next day the opposition removed the remaining piling of the "wood dock"—so-called though no wood was ever placed there.

In the next low-water period following completion of No. 1, Sams had Tommy Davidson drive piles for Scow Wheel No. 2 at the north end of Ives Island. This wheel also was under contract to McGowan. Braces angling downstream supported the 150-foot inside lead and the 200-foot outside fence of this classical twin rear-boom type scow—which was constructed by the Joseph Supples' Shipyard in Portland.

Sams' Wheel No. 1 and the Bailey Gatzert *about 1908. (William Sams, II)*

Sams' Wheel No. 2 was 8 feet wide and some 28 feet in diameter, with curved dips. These dips were not natural "crooks"—known as "knees" and cut from a tree—but sawed from lumber. A bullwheel windlass mounted on the lower part of the gins made it fairly easy to raise and lower the rotor. Cables in fairleads ran over the tops of the gins and wound around the shaft of the bullwheel.

About 1902, Sams was coerced by his "friend," Captain Ives, into the unprofitable venture of building another twin-boom, 28x8-foot scow dipper on Ives Island, 1,000 feet, as specified by law, upstream from the Paquet Wheel. When Sams protested against the suggestion, Captain Ives threatened to lease the site to someone else; therefore, to protect his No. 2 wheel at the upper end of the island, Sams was forced to erect the unwanted No. 3 structure. For the parts, he purchased the near-barren Koch and Ladzic scow and lead downstream on Pierce Island, and moved these to the site specified by Ives. Landowners on whose property the wheels were located commonly received a fourth of the receipts.

Construction aides were Frank Estabrook, John Baughman, Johnny Stiquin, Peter McGuff, and Charley Minor. Much difficult and tedious pick-and-shovel labor was involved in digging the 250-foot trench in which to imbed or anchor the mudsill of the lower Ives Island wheel lead. Bill Sams, who also aided in this excavation, still groans at the memory of moving those multiple tons of gravel to attain a ditch 6 to 7 feet deep. Ives' choice of location was not good, though, and the "show" was soon abandoned. The scow was sold to some forgotten investor, and the piling rotted away in ten or so years.

Billy Butler's Saloon, farm, and landing, about 1908 (now Skamania Landing). Mc-Gowan's Cannery can be seen across the river. (John Butler)

First school at Skamania, Washington, 1906. Captain Sherman Ives (man with beard) was visiting the school. From left: *Mrs. William Sams, Sr., Minnie Sams, George Extle (on horse), Mary Extle, Amy Leavens, Esther Lindstrom, Mrs. Yettick, Lucy Butler, Leona Sams, Captain Ives, Charles Murray, Bob Sams, Fred Sams, and Robbie Yettick.*

At the start of his fishing endeavor, Sams sold fish from the catamaran wheel to the Warrendale Cannery, but the cannery men grumbled about the "dry, sunburned" fish. McGowan, with whom Sams later had a contract, did not complain. After the contract with McGowan expired in 1903, he sold his fish to the Rooster Rock Cannery at a higher price. A cannery pickup boat was sent each day to get them.

Sams sold his No. 1 site and stationary wheel to the Columbia River Packers Association (CRPA) in 1910. With proceeds from the sale of the stationary and the scow wheels, he purchased a ranch of 110 acres at Skamania, Washington, overlooking the once-rushing waters where he had operated his wheels. There, with his brother, Leo, he retired from the fishwheel business and became a net fisherman and merchant. However, his son, Bill, who had been employed at Warren's Cannery since 1905, continued on there.

A succession of new operators could not make the No. 1 pay, and in 1921, it was practically given to Eric Enquist, who kept it running profitably until wheels were stopped by law. The agreement was that the CRPA, who owned the property, would continue to pay taxes for the wheel site; also the license for the wheel. In return Enquist was to sell the fish to the company, but he was to be paid full market value for the fish. Enquist improved the wheel by closing several holes in the lead during low water, and by constructing an incline-plane barrier of closely spaced steel rails in the dipway to force the fish into the sweep of the dips.

FISHWHEEL WEBBING

Sams had made all of his own wire webbing, using No. 9 wire for the bottoms of the dips, and No. 11 for the sides. During the great run of smelt in 1899, the dippers of his Ives Island scow scooped up hundreds of them, but almost all of them fell back through the 4-inch mesh wire. Only a few slid from the discharge troughs down the long, wet chute leading from the axle to the scow-deck fish bin. However, it was salmon that Sams wanted for sale to the canneries, not smelt.

Before the wire webbing, there had been willow webbing. The ancient art of basketry extended to fishwheel dip webbing and mesh. Willow baskets attached to the rim of some of the first recorded European wheels served as fish dippers. Roy Fure, of Alaska, told how some of the remoter Alaskan Eskimos and Indians used a coarse willow fabric on their fishwheel dips; also how a peculiar knot was used to secure the willow web and prevent its slipping. U. S. Fish and Wildlife Service correspondents from Alaska have corroborated the use of willow fishwheel dip covering.

Columbia River Gorge Indians made nets from selected wild flax and other plant fibers long before the white man began fishing this mighty stream. The natives, though, did not build fishwheels until some time after they had been introduced by Samuel Wilson. Wilson used dipnet twine on the bottom and small thin slats on the sides of the scoops for construction of the first fishwheel on the Columbia River in 1879. When Thornton Williams chose to copy Samuel Wilson's fishwheel, he ordered handwoven "Chinese" wire from San Francisco for dip covering. The 2-inch mesh was identical to that installed along the railing of steamboats "to keep people from falling overboard." Williams placed the same material on the sides and bottom of his dips. Some of the early web was galvanized after weaving. In the galvanizing process, zinc soldered the joints where the wires were twisted together and made them solid.

A distinction must be noted between two types of handmade dipper material. One was the so-called chicken-wire design, usually formed in a diamond pattern; the other was the superior double-twist hexagonal Chinese web. Each was used concurrently by different operators, and in the course of time both were woven by Columbia River men; however, the double-twist type gradually supplanted the chicken wire.

They found the 20-gauge poultry-wire fishwheel baskets were not strong enough to withstand the inexorable force and vibration of the Columbia, although some Canadian and Alaskan Indians found them satisfactory on their smaller installations. Early in the history of the fishwheels, Reuben Snow, of Lower Cascades, learned to make the chicken-wire weave. He did the twisting by hand.

At first Snow was secretive, but he later permitted his employee, Leo Sams (brother of William Sams, Sr.) to learn the process. Sams subsequently set up shop in his barn to "knit" this "lace." In the beginning he twisted the heavy Nos. 8 and 9 wire by hand, but later used strong pliers to tighten the turns. Thereafter, in process of evolution, Sams forged heavy blacksmith tongs with "V" notches to grasp the two wires for even tighter twisting.

Leo's weaving bench was essentially the same for both kinds of plaiting except that the framework for the poultry type did not have the crossbar with separators underneath. Each strand for this pattern was kept in a small coil and unwound as needed to permit turning. Instead of passing over and under (as cloth fabric is woven) the wires were turned first by hand, then with pliers, about the adjacent members. In this process, 24 to 32 individual rolls had to be juggled and kept free from tangling. Reuben Snow and Myron Kelly were the only wheel men in the Cascades area who persisted in making this style.

Although the discovery and weaving of "chicken wire" in the Cascades region was a boon to wheel men, they soon learned its shortcomings. It was too loose; flexing and abrasion at joints caused the wires to snap. But Warren's men were constantly experimenting in their shops on Bradford Island, seeking to devise sturdier wheel fittings. Sometime in the late nineties one of the Swedes untwisted a piece of the "Oriental web" and learned how to make it by hand. Leo and William Sams did likewise, and from that time on, no more Chinese wire was brought to the Cascades from San Francisco.

Left: *Weaving Chinese-type fishwheel wire. Note that the open slot of case-hardened endpiece of twisting brace has been lowered over one warp line, and operator is ready to carry brace under and around warp line to make a secure twist.* Right: *Vise and storage arrangement for Chinese-type fishwheel webbing. Vise is open so that completed mesh can be moved through opening away from operator. The upper element of vise is then lowered and tightened to clamp warp wires securely before another pass (to left in this case) is made with the brace and weft wire bobbin. A side line welt is in process of formation.*

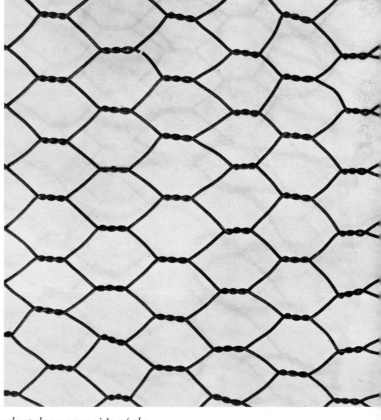

Left: *This view of William Sams weaving shows completed meshwork on near side of the weaving vise, later to be coiled on two white boards. The frame, twisting brace, and completed wire are now in Oregon Historical Society Museum.* Right: *Poultry-wire type weave of fishwheel wire. This web was less durable than the Chinese type.*

RIVER TRANSPORTATION

Parsimonious Captain Ives—who stored his gold pieces at home in a stocking hung on a nail—was an expert at hauling freight under sail upriver from Portland and Vancouver. At the Cascades he employed resident Indians to man the towlines for pulling boats through the very swift water as far as the Washington shore landing just below the rapids. Although he often boasted, "I'd get out my headache stick and then the Indians would really pull," there is no witness to this act or to his ability to maneuver his craft at the same time he applied the club to the Indians. Eric Enquist said that Captain Ives and Joseph Latourell took schooners or sailing scows up over the Cascade Rapids, with numerous Indians pulling lines and twisting capstans. Sails were ineffective for upstream navigation against an east wind and the swift current. Nor was tacking back and forth practical under these conditions in the narrow confines of the Lower Cascades.

Steam had been introduced prior to the heyday of the wheel era, but there is no record of small power boats earlier than the 1880s. Surely some must have been used with the cask fish floats prior to 1889 when Warren operated the *Sakana* and *Quinatt*, each about 35 feet long and equipped with upright wood-burning steam boilers.

The famous *Nerka*, brought into service about 1892, was the first adequate salmon pickup boat at the Cascades, replacing both the *Sakana* and *Quinatt* which were smaller. She had a length of about 46 feet, beam of 10 feet, a Scotch marine wood-burn-

Wilavis-Nerka *race with the* Wilavis *ahead. Butler's Eddy and Billy Butler's buildings are across the river. (John Butler)*

56

ing boiler amidships, and a canopy cover from bow to stern. The exhaust was discharged by a tube up the smokestack to increase draft on the firebox. She was remodeled from a fantail to square stern in 1905, and continued in service until around 1916, when replaced by the internal combustion-powered boats *Warco* (diesel), *Hornet* (gas), the converted *Sakana* (gas), and the B-4, all owned by the Warren Packing Company—for which title the word *Warco* is an abbreviation.

The *Wilavis* was built in Portland about 1900 by a Mr. Smith, who named it for his son Will and daughter Avis. This was a well-designed and carefully wrought craft with a silent 3-cylinder, triple-expansion steam engine, tube boiler with condenser, and reinjector. The *Georgiana*, a propeller-passenger boat, had the same type of engine. The Columbia River Packers Association engaged the *Wilavis* as a pickup boat to haul fish from their net operation sites, and from wheels between Bonneville and their Rooster Rock Cannery, then to Ellsworth, Washington, when the cannery was moved to the latter location. The *Wilavis* would "lay up" over night at the upper end of its run and leave early in the morning for the cannery, picking up fish along the way.

Many races are recorded between the sternwheelers on the Columbia. Lesser craft also had their supporters. The *Wilavis* was admired by all who saw her, and the envy of those who knew boats. The *Nerka*, swinging a 36-inch propeller and powered by an 8-inch single cylinder, 11-inch stroke engine, was no derelict. Many impromptu races resulted between the two craft. It was commonly believed that the skipper of the *Wilavis* deliberately lost enough of these sprints to generate enthusiasm for a money match. Eventually a real contest was agreed upon to extend from Bonneville to a point abreast McGowan's Cannery.

On a bright July day in 1903, George Warren, with a $20 stake on the *Nerka*, dropped his hat to signal the start. With the initial thrust of propellers they began their frantic rush downriver. First one was in the lead, then the other, but there was a difference in skippers. Each time the *Nerka* forged ahead, her over-confident captain, Charley Yettick, released steam pressure in wild whistles of triumph; but Smith, who piloted the *Wilavis*, did not deign to waste power in this manner.

Steam energy from the boiler on the *Wilavis* was used in three successively lower-pressure cylinders. The exhausted steam then traveled to a condenser and was returned to the boiler, where it was used over and over. However, in the case of the *Nerka*, steam went up the stack as exhaust and was lost.

Midway in the race, the *Nerka* boiler ran low on water. Fireman Fred Miller then permitted the fire to burn low while adding cold water, and by so doing lost pressure. Desperately he fed kindling into the firebox attempting to regain steam, but by this time the race was already lost. The *Wilavis* finished a length ahead. The last captain of the *Wilavis* was Lacey Wing from the highlands above Cape Horn, approximately eight miles downriver from Skamania, Washington. The *Nerka* had been designed for quick, short runs, and while she performed these tasks admirably, she could not sustain sprinting speed.

Bill Sams told of an amusing incident involving the *Nerka*, which took place when John Nixon, her skipper, attempted to aid the *Keystone*. Three boats became involved in the melee, the *Nerka*, McGowan's *Keystone*, and the CRPA *Triton*, piloted by Percy Simons. The *Triton* had picked up fish from Sams' No. 2 Wheel on Ives Island, and had started downstream when the engine died. She drifted westward, barely missing the Paquet Wheel, and ran aground at a point opposite Pierce Island Bar.

From aboard the *Nerka*, Nixon had observed the accident and resolved to pull the rival boat back to the main river against the current. A piece of wood tied to a towline was floated from the *Nerka* toward the *Triton*, but the rope proved too short. John edged closer and closer to shore until the *Nerka's* rear keel hit bottom, whereupon the current caught her bow, swinging her crosswise with the bar. If Nixon had applied full reverse, he could have backed her off, but he tried to swing the prow against the current with full speed ahead and succeeded only in ramming into the stern of the *Triton*, shoving it a boat-length farther onto the gravel. The *Nerka*, drawing about 4 feet of water, then heeled over and stopped with her stem under the *Triton's* afterdeck.

Nixon had run the engine ahead all the way in but later tried alternately placing it in forward and reverse, finally leaving it reversed. In disgust he dashed his old derby hat to the deck and stomped on it. Although plenty of water registered in the gauge, in a frenzy he pumped the boiler full until there was no more steam. Only water spouted from the whistle when he attempted to signal to the *Keystone*. Meanwhile, the skipper of the *Keystone* had seen the mess, and because his craft drew less water, had guided it through the Greenhorn-Suck (channel) below Pierce Island, where he could approach the scene from below.

Bill Sams, fireman on the *Nerka* at this time, went aboard the rescue ship to handle the towline. The *Triton* came off easily and soon her engine was started—but liberation of the *Nerka* was a different story. The towline cinched up so tightly around the *Triton's* towing bitt that water oozed from the wood. Finally the grounded *Nerka* began moving toward deep water. By the time a line was attached, Nixon had blown some water out of the boiler and developed enough steam to swing the propeller, but in his excitement he did not realize he had left the system in reverse, opposing the *Keystone*.

The *Nerka's* screw, churning violently in the wrong direction, ploughed a foot-deep furrow which remained visible for several years in the tightly packed gravel of the bar. Upon reaching deep water once more, Nixon exulted, "We'd never have made it if the *Nerka* hadn't been pulling too." He did not realize his boat propeller was opposing that of the rescue vessel, nor did he ever admit the reason for the loss of 6 inches of brass worn from the screw, despite its having to be sent to Portland for repair.

Although he was entrusted to skipper the *Nerka*, John Nixon was no boatman. His associates could begin to relax only after his usual two or three accidents per year. One time, early in 1906, with Frank Warren, Sr., and his namesake son aboard the *Nerka*, Nixon came into the cannery dock at considerable speed and rammed the dock with enough force to send the two Warrens sprawling toward the bow of the craft. While recovering their footing, they scrutinized Nixon speculatively, then quickly clambered up into the cannery, whereupon Nixon turned to his fireman and blurted:

"Yesus Krist. Did you see dere eyes? Dey vas vite!"

FISHWHEEL LEADS

Efforts to increase the catch of individual wheels were centered chiefly on fences or leads of several forms, including rock fences, rock cuts or channels, and vertical and horizontal bars. Some leads were crude and others were elaborate. Thoughts of conservation certainly did not govern length of fishwheel leads in the early days, but later, laws were passed limiting fences to a third of the river's width; otherwise smaller rivers like the Sandy might have been completely blocked. At one time, three wheels existed on the Sandy.

Before the John Day Dam forebay was raised, April 16-20, 1968, Emory Strong, in his book, *Stone Age on the Columbia*, told how he could still see an Indian fish lead made of stone at Fountain Bar, about 14 miles east of the mouth of the John Day River. This was constructed to guide salmon toward a low cliff where they could easily be netted in high water.

Where the river turned almost on edge near The Dalles, it was not always possible to install fences, nor blast channels, but the extremely swift water through the Long Narrows caused fish to travel near the vertical lava walls where irregularities in the rock surface slowed the current somewhat, allowing the fish to ascend with less effort. In the channel between Grave and Wasco islands above The Dalles, they sometimes frequented the large, rounded, and deep holes which had been worn into the lava by grinding action of loose stones swirling endlessly through the centuries. Dipnetters soon learned of these areas and reaped an easy harvest.

At the Cascades, blueback salmon, which customarily swim near the surface, were more susceptible to deflection by leads to areas where they could readily be taken by fishwheels or dipnets. Evidently the need for guides was discovered very early in the evolution of the Cascade wheels. Thornton Williams wrote to his brother in 1880, explaining the need for a "drift" fence. Photos taken prior to 1890 show a vertical picket deflector serving the Williams Wheel, similar to fish weirs now used by various hatcherymen on streams of the Northwest. This type of fence consisted of timber tripod "horses" or dolphins weighted down with rocks placed on a platform (situated in the lower third of the three-legged structures), and two heavy timbers extending laterally between the many dolphins.

Innumerable 2x2 or 3x3 timber pickets, or round poles, were set as deeply as possible into the river bed (leaving three inches of space between to permit passage of water). These were nailed to the two connecting timbers, on stringers, with the tops of the paling members leaning downstream at a 45- to

60-degree angle. These guides could be erected only in shallow water; they were not adapted to wide, river-level fluctuations, and were not self-cleaning as were horizontal bars. Frequent rakings were necessary to rid them of debris.

The submersible horizontal-bar weirs were ingenious, illustrating a high degree of adaptation to conditions created by the rock rubble of the great Cascade Slide and the Eagle Creek geological formation. Rivermen are emphatic in proclaiming their superiority over the vertical picket arrangement. They could be installed in relatively deep water when necessary, and would rid themselves of floating debris, yet direct fish to the wheel dips. Apparently the piling on the downstream side of the horizontal bars did not seriously impede the movement of adult salmon along the bars to the dipway.

A horizontal-bar lead—approximately 100 feet long and heavily buttressed by large stones—angled downstream from Warren's Stationary 3 Wheel, which he considered the "backbone" of his success. The stones of this lead are still very prominent. Handmade wire webbing and iron straps, as well as base logs imbedded in the rocks, can also be found at the site on the Washington shore opposite the downstream end of Bradford Island. According to Eric Enquist, No. 3 was not washed away—"time just gnawed it away. After maintenance was stopped, the big rocks held the foundation in place." The dipway was placed 10 to 20 feet above low-water level, making this a spring chinook and blueback wheel.

FISHWHEEL "PIRATES"

About 1937, during construction of Bonneville Dam, some local adventurers visited Warren's No. 3 seeking salmon. Though operations had been prohibited since 1935, the hoist was still operable, and they lowered the dippers into the water. Soon a number of fine chinooks were flopping in the fish box. As the fishermen prepared to depart with their prizes, a well-known Washington State Department of Fisheries inspector, who had been trying for months to apprehend the fish "pirates," stormed onto the scene and triumphantly took them into custody. Nevertheless the men pleaded "not guilty," engaging for their defense a man of jurisprudence known to every citizen of Stevenson, Washington.

At the trial they told, with injured dignity, of having innocently boarded the strange machine on the river bank, and in attempting to learn its purpose, had pulled a lever which, to their "complete amazement," caused something to turn, bringing struggling fish from the river. While they were engaged in righteous endeavors to stop the dipper and help the salmon back into the safety of the water, the belligerent game warden arrived and arrested the honorable citizens. Duly impressed, the court acquitted those so wrongly accused! The Fisheries inspector still grows explosive when this story is related, although the defense lawyer readily admits his clients' guilt. Now in retirement, he is still greatly amused by the incident.

After completion of the Cascade Locks in 1896, the Washington Portage Railway was used only to haul salmon from the Warren wheels, which included Stationary 2, Scows 3 and 15, as well as the scow and two stationary wheels at Cascade Rapids. Following relocation of the Cascades Railroad line in 1907, a horse, and later an automobile (remodeled into a gasoline-powered locomotive) transported the fish from the Washington wheels. At Moffett's Landing the individual fish were skidded down a wetted plank chute aboard the *Nerka*, where Bill Sams and John Nixon placed them in the compartments of the craft for transport downstream and across the river to the cannery at Warrendale. The catch from each wheel was kept in separate units by large pieces of burlap or canvas, and each unit was weighed individually at the cannery.

One time in the early 1900s, Earl J. Warren (no kin to the fish-packing company Warrens) and Herb Turner pumped a handcar up to Stevenson from Skamania. En route back, they stopped at an untended (but operating) wheel near the site of the old town of Lower Cascades, Washington Territory. As they watched the spring chinooks sliding from the dips into the locked fish house, the idea occurred to them to "borrow" a few for their own use. Since they could not break the lock, they decided to stop the wheel by thrusting a pole across the dipway upstream from the axle.

Cascade Locks construction, looking downstream, December 1, 1883. (Russ Nichols and Wayne Gurley)

May 24, 1893 view from Cascade Locks before completion of the navigation facility on canal. Note the portage railroad incline across the river close to the Washington shore. (U. S. Corps of Engineers)

Navigation locks at Cascade Locks, Oregon. Piling shown in left background is a portion of the "incline" or upper terminal of Cascades Portage Railway on Washington shore. (William Sams, II)

Stationary 19, Cascade Rapids, Cascade Locks. Photo shows landing above the wheel where fish were loaded onto the portage railroad car. (John Wachter)

Steamer Tahoma *and the McGowan double fishwheel, May 9, 1914. Cascade Navigation Locks is in the distance (mid-photo) and the town of Stevenson, Washington is on the left. Note portage railroad trestle at left. (Vera Sprague)*

McGowan double wheel downstream from Cascade Locks on the Oregon shore. (Dorothy P. Nile)

It is not known whether Turner actually entered the fish house through the dipper chute and was attempting to exit when the pole broke—allowing the wheel to revolve again—but it is known that he was carried around the axle one or more times. He was nearly scalped before Earl Warren managed to stop the machine and rescue his bleeding companion. In Warren's haste to sew and save Turner's torn and loosened scalp, the fish were forgotten.

Bud Cates suffered a similar mishap about 1907 at the McGowan Wheel below Cascade Locks, when he leaned too far out over the dipway and his forelock was torn loose by one of the dipper arms. Luckily, the local doctor at Cascade Locks managed to replace his head of hair.

When Bonneville Dam construction was started in 1933, Perry Kitzmiller had a narrow escape. He had gained a berth as boat operator for the Corps of Engineers, shuttling men back and forth across the river to the Washington side, on a narrow, cranky craft, the *Ocia*. He came to grief when the engine quit, causing him to be swept into the dipway of Stationary 2. Fortunately the rotor was raised and not turning; otherwise a more harrowing tale would have been told. Bill Sams' comment on the incident was: "It is very doubtful if a boat could actually go through a wheel, even if there were enough water to turn it. Unless timing was just right, the dip would come down on top of the boat and either sink it or stop the rotor."

THE WARREN WHEELS

Warren's method of getting fish from Scows 3 and 15 was by high line. A single cable about an inch in diameter stretched from the framework upon the bank; the other end was securely fastened to the scow. A sort of wheel carriage was run on this one-inch cable, with a smaller cable fastened to the carrier, and the hand-operated winch to pull up the loaded fish boxes of regular size. Fish were collected by the Portage Railway crew and shipped each morning by the Washington Portage Railway on the north bank.

Warren placed Scow 15 and lead approximately one-fourth mile upstream from his Stationary No. 2, on the Washington shore west of Government Slide. It was a standard-size scow wheel constructed by his "Swedes" about 1895, and it had the characteristic finished appearance of all the Warren wheels and leads, complete with walkway on top. The 150-foot lead had two dipways, and a customary wheel tender's shack was located on the bank above.

Al Hendricks, Gus Cook, and Andrew Jackson tended this wheel for a time. One morning Jackson found two strange fish in the scow bottom— one about 14 inches long, the other 12 inches—and carried them to John Nixon, operator of the *Nerka*, who exclaimed:

"Vot are dese tamn tings? Are dese good to eat?

Vould you eat dem?" Nixon identified them as bass and assured Jackson they were fine, edible fish, but Jackson retorted:

"Vell, you take da tamn tings." So, Nixon enjoyed a fine bass feed.

Chinook and blueback salmon, however, were the chief species taken by No. 15, and they were collected each day by the Portage Railway crew.

Scow 3—erected shortly after the 1894 flood—took chinooks, bluebacks, steelhead, and the usual noncommercial species. Shad were also taken but given away by the innocent wheel tender to a person who sold them to Warren's Cannery. The Warren Packing Company did not bother to process shad taken by its own wheels, but would purchase them from outsiders at a low price to induce the "independents" to sell salmon to their cannery.

A tale told of this wheel is that one July day in 1896 it nearly swamped from weight of bluebacks. While the lower river fishermen were on strike and unimpeded by nets, the blueback came "like smelt" so thickly that all one could see below the wheel was their backs sticking out of the water. They swarmed into the scoops of the wheel in such numbers that it was necessary for Al Hendricks to raise the dips above the water to prevent foundering and disaster.

Some of the Scow 3 tenders were John Brask, Matt Hanlon, Andrew Freeman, Al Hendricks, Andrew Jackson, Ed Cook, John Cook, Gus Cook, and Emil Strandholm. Al, the gentle Swede, did not join the Warren crew until after 1896.

Scows 3 and 15 operated profitably until they were outlawed in Washington. It is interesting to note that Scow 3 was located at the approximate site where pioneer Samuel Wilson raised the first wheel on the Columbia—described in the trial records as a few hundred feet to the east of Government Slide, near Fort Rains. But, in contrast to Warren's experience, Samuel Wilson never made a nickel from his handiwork. Nor did he anticipate that expensive legal maneuvers would result from the struggle to prevent Thornton Williams from keeping his patent.

Stationary 19 rotor being moved up onto the bank away from river at flood stage. Crib is completely inundated. Al Hendricks is shown on cross-member at right holding young Runar. Mrs. Hendricks stands nearby holding Roy. Note the carriage within the gins bearing weight of the rotor. The capstan is acting as winch to move the structure. (Al Hendricks)

THE STEVENSON BROTHERS

The "city" of Upper Cascades, Washington Territory, was once known as Bagdad; Carson Landing was once called "Sprague," and the Carson Springs area "Ash." If the cluster of buildings opposite Cascade Locks had any other name before that of Stevenson, it has not been revealed—unless it was "Sheppard's Point," after the Sheppard's donation land grant. However, when the two brothers, George and Momen Stevenson, gave land and office space for the Skamania County seat (moved from Lower Cascades, Washington Territory, in 1893), "Stevenson" became official. Activities of these two brothers encompassed the Portage Railroad, fishwheels, land, and public service, none of which can rightly be separated from the others in a brief history of the town.

Although the Washington Cascade Portage Railroad was virtually abandoned by December 19, 1890, the Union Pacific retained ownership and made a 2-hour run each day transporting fish downstream to Moffett's Landing (later North Bonneville). George Stevenson was assigned by the railroad company to manage this operation, but acting as a state legislator, was often absent from Skamania County, and at various times employed S. B. Jones or Frank Estabrook to take over for him. Momen Stevenson, a Washington state senator, spent even less time in the vicinity than his brother.

Following S. B. Jones's death, Estabrook was assigned to run the locomotive as well as the two Stevenson-owned scow fishwheels, which were located just below Cascade Rapids on the Washington side of the river. Both scows leaked badly and considerable time was required to man the crude pumps. To bail the water and keep up with his other duties during the absence of the lawmaker, Estabrook developed two paddle-wheel, square bilge pumps. When George hurriedly returned to his wheels at the close of one legislative session, he was both surprised and relieved to find his two scows still afloat, the two river-powered bilge pumps working perfectly while his handy man puttered about at odd chores.

Estabrook told how fishermen shipped smaller sturgeon concealed under other species in the fishboxes, although a 3-year closed season was imposed on these fish around 1903. He also remembered the 10-foot sturgeon which somehow came down the wheel chute into one of the Stevenson scows and required three men to remove it. How such a large fish could exit from the dippers, turn at right angles into the long delivery chute, and slide down into the barge was not explained, and still remains puzzling.

Upper Cascades on the Columbia, 1867, by C. E. Watkins—showing one of the new locomotives, Bush's Hotel in the background, and the Oneonta *across the bay. (Marjorie Shantz)*

Left: *Steamer* Oneonta, *Upper Cascades, Washington Territory, 1867. Fort Lugenbeel is seen on the hill in background above the town or portage railroad terminus of Upper Cascades. (Marjorie Shantz).* Right: *Fort Lugenbeel, the upper blockhouse. (Dr. George Beck)*

Left: *Saloon below the blockhouse near Middle Landing, Washington shore. Note Cascades Portage Railroad grade at left.* Right: *Original middle blockhouse, Cascades, 1867, at Fort Rains near Middle Landing. (Marjorie Shantz)*

Lower Cascades, Washington terminus of the Cascades Railroad in 1867, on bank of Columbia opposite Warrendale. Locomotive in middle of picture was the "Betsy." (Oregon Historical Society)

Steamer Cascade *at Lower Landing on the south side of Hamilton Island, 1865. Note the S. M. Hamilton farm buildings. This western terminus was built in 1862-63 and came into use April 20, 1863. Incline and wharf boats are shown in practically new condition; all were destroyed by the 1894 flood. (Ruth Guppy)*

67

Cascade Rapids and Bridge of the Gods, 1935, prior to closure of Bonneville Dam. Note the lakes of the Wauna area on top of Cascade Slide at left. Old Skamania County road winds white (upper left) around Ash's meadow, then east to southern tip of slide. Cascade Navigation Locks is shown bypassing the rapids. (U. S. Corps of Engineers)

No. 16—"THE BIG WHEEL"

To citizens of Stevenson, Warren's No. 16 was "The Big Wheel" because it was the first one west of the town and the most imposing device of its kind on the lower river. After 1894, the portage railway ended there. Picnickers visited the area frequently during late summer and fall after water had receded from the dipway. As with the Phelps and other wheels at The Dalles and Cascades regions, the more adventurous young people would enter the dips and ride around in the improvised "ferris wheel." One near-tragedy, though, is recalled. Johnny Baughman, grandson of the famed steamboat captain, Ephraim W. Baughman, fell from a dip and was mauled between a descending crossarm and the dipway floor. Wayne Mann and Sid Suckow carried the young man to medical aid. Bill Iman recalled: "His head was mashed out of shape and eyes swelled shut, but he lived."

Many residents of the Skamania County seat have fond memories of "stealing" fish from "The Big Wheel," and stories are also gleefully told of posting a lookout to warn of the game warden's approach, then snagging salmon from below the dipway. Some old-timers in Stevenson even admitted lowering the wheel at night during weekend closure periods to gain a bonanza of migrant fish.

Lloyd Marsh and others who arrived on the scene late in the age of fishwheels recall seeing the receiving house overflowing with salmon. Because it was so profitable, No. 16 was carefully tended until all wheels were banned in Washington. Reservoir-clearing crews destroyed this "monument" in a year or so, and the site was later flooded as Bonneville Lake waters were raised to an elevation of 68 feet in February 1938.

Warren's Swedes had imbedded Stationary 16 in the Washington shore, where the Columbia began its tumultuous race over Cascade Rapids. A scow wheel had been used to test the location before they risked the greater expenditure of a permanent structure. This was the easternmost of the Warren stationary wheels. Designed ruggedly to withstand the river's surge, the log crib was reinforced with piling firmly set in the rubble of Cascade Slide.

CASCADE SLIDE

Importance of the Cascade Slide cannot be minimized in this story of fishwheels, for it created the rapids and swift water, below which operation and development of the original fishwheels on the Columbia was made possible. In the slack water created from the Cascades east to The Dalles, no wheels could operate successfully because of lack of current. Only at Salmon Island and on the solid conglomerate of the Eagle Creek Formation between Tanner and McCord creeks could a firm foundation for wheels be found on the Oregon shore. There was no solid rock on the Washington side of the Cascades; hence, crib-type wheels were necessary there.

Geologists who have studied the Columbia River Gorge for decades tell how the river washed away a portion of the dam created by the great Cascade Slide, depositing much of this detritus to form the several islands below the rapids, namely, Hamilton, Ives, and Pierce. A vast amount of slide material between Cascade Locks and Ruckel Creek—called the Ruckel Slide—was pushed up onto the Oregon shore by the vast inertia of the avalanche, traveling at a speed of possibly 100 or more miles per hour. This slide material blocked the drainage from the talus slope and caused the water to rise until it began pushing slide material back into the river. The result was a moving, insecure formation upon which wheel cribs, railroads, and highways could not be anchored safely.

Ruckel Slide's "reverse" motion was later stabilized by two series of drainage tunnels driven back through the clay and the boulder avalanche material to the loose rock debris. One set of drain tubes was described as a "rabbit warren" of holes wandering hither and yon, excavated between 1918 and

1923 by the Union Pacific. The second set was dug and shored to precise specifications (1935-36) by the U. S. Army, Corps of Engineers men when Bonneville Dam was under construction. H. R. "Bob" Moore, who later became a highly esteemed fishway superintendent at the dam, tells of torrential flows of water suddenly breaking into the drain tunnels that he and his associates were excavating.

On one occasion, Bob Moore, Floyd McFarren, and Jim Wickham had most urgent need to flee from a great outburst of water, which rose to a depth of 3 feet in their 6-foot-high tunnel, but flight was delayed for an unexpected reason: Jim Wickham was "all shoulders and no hips," and customarily wore no belt. When the sudden onslaught of water "as if from a giant pump" nearly swept them off their feet, Jim's trousers slipped down around his ankles and hobbled him so seriously he could not run to safety. Jim finally managed to retrieve his trousers and all made it to safety. The water flow continued for many days before the pocket was finally drained.

CONSTRUCTION AND OPERATION

Stones or boulders from the Cascade Slide were plentiful along the beaches where Warren's wheels were located. From the crane a workman would pull out the hook and wooden line (riggers of a generation or two ago knew Manila or sisal rope as "wooden") which he attached to a heavy chain secured about a large rock. By winch the boulder was dragged to the derrick, then lifted over the side into the enclosure formed by the wheel cribwork of notched and drift-pinned logs. Special temporary tracks were used on occasion to move stones to the winch. Hand operation in this manner was slow, but laborers received only $2 per 10-hour day. However, the low pay scale made it possible to keep experienced laborers employed until the next fishing season.

Although Fred Sams—Bill Sams' brother—observed "there were damn few rocks a couple of Warren's Swedes could not lift," placement of stones and cribbing logs was difficult. To raise the heavy logs, rocks, and timbers of a wheel, the Warren crews fabricated a stiff leg derrick similar to those employed in lifting and placing the closely fitted stones of the Cascade Navigation Locks. These classical hoisting machines were common before the age of steam- and gasoline-powered cranes.

Steam power, other than by locomotive or stern-wheeler, was first applied at the Cascades sometime between 1876 and 1900 in construction of Cascade Navigation Locks. But on fishwheels it was first employed when Warren's crew started to rebuild Stationary No. 2 immediately after the 1894 flood. A small steam (donkey) boiler and winch unit was moved to the wheel site on the cannery scow. John Nixon, who later became cannery superintendent, operated this steam winch to lift the stones into their proper place. Auxiliary lines, pulled by one or more of the crew, swung the boom. A blacksmith was constantly employed by Warren to form the myriads of "U" bolts, metal rings, fittings, and long pins needed in fabricating his fishwheels.

Unlike Warren's men, many wheel builders were "wood butchers," scrambling odds and ends of lumber and screen into "turning rigs" which might catch a fish or two, or hopefully, a fortune.

Almost all wheel operators have recorded the revolutions per minute of their machines. These rates varied from less than 2 turns per minute to the excessive 12 rotations per minute by the Seufert Cement Wheel in The Dalles area. The excessive speed of the Cement Wheel was later corrected by placement of horizontal concrete baffles across the dipway channel upstream from the dippers, thus slowing the current sufficiently to make this wheel one of the top producers on the river. A speed of 3 to 5 revolutions per minute was ideal. Loss from excessive speed, though, could be offset by the greater catch from swift water; one could afford to lose a few when many fish were captured.

There has never been a report of a wheel at the Cascades turning fast enough to throw the fish over the discharge trough, but there have been a few "rambunctious" steelhead that hit the bottom of the chute on their tails and jumped over the axle to escape. Occasionally in slow- or fast-moving wheels a fish did not get out in time, especially if it landed at the far end and was slow in flopping. Sometimes a larger salmon which landed with its head toward the upper end of the chute would lie on its belly, continue a swimming motion, and remain there until the wheel had turned past the discharge opening.

Operation and maintenance of the wheels were demanding tasks. Constant vigilance was necessary to keep the rotors running true in their dipway and at proper depth. Fish trapped by the dippers would be lost if river water was permitted to rise above the axle. Bearings required lubrication, and constant repairs were necessary to resist the ravages of rot, insects, and the relentless assault of the river. Wheels were disassembled and repaired in the winter during low-water period. The erection of a typical Warren stationary wheel required the services of approximately six or eight men for five to seven months, depending on the location, conditions, and difficulties.

SOUNDS OF WHEELS

It seems doubtful that noises emanating from a wheel actually affected fish approaching from far downstream, but wheel men generally were convinced that noise should be eliminated if possible. Certainly some wheels produced more noise than others. Each had distinctive sounds influenced by construction details and differences in the existing currents.

Eric Enquist, who sometimes slept at his wheels, recalled that during the semi-silence of night, above the murmur and hiss of the wire meshes, he could hear the splash of the crosspieces entering the water. As the dips came up, water which had been carried above the surface fell back with a distinctive rustle. Strange groans, squeaks, creaks, thumps, and quivers could be heard or felt. As a big salmon came down the discharge chute into the fish box, the heavy thud of landing was plainly audible, followed by wild thrashings. Soon the fish tired, fell on its side, and slapped spasmodically until the end brought silence. On still days and nights, when sounds carried far, Enquist said he could hear and distinguish between two different wheels operating on the opposite (Washington) shore.

There was another, and ominous, sound related to fishwheels. Flood waters carried many logs downstream—and occasionally into the dipway of a fishwheel. "When one hit, the crash was sickening," Enquist said. Reconstruction had to wait until daylight, as only kerosene lanterns were available to examine the damage, and their wan light could not dispel the danger. Logs would also strike against the lead, then grind along the horizontal bars to the outboard end, where the current whipped them on downriver.

On occasion, unoiled axles shattered the peace of the river with their screechings. Bill Sams told of precarious climbs over a wheel to pour oil into the bearing cups. He had to walk out on the projecting twin scow booms above the curling water, preferably when the rotor was stopped. If the bearings became dry while the machine was fishing, lubrication was even more dangerous, as one could be swept overboard by the moving dips—and life jackets were unknown. Every time a dip came out of the water, the rising weight would pitch the stern downward, causing the bow of a scow wheel to rear up like a "bucking broncho." To cross the dipway of a stationary wheel at either end on a structural timber and reach the bearing carriage on the outside of the crib above the churning river was no job for a "dizzy-head."

Sudden and great fluctuations of water levels were common on the Columbia. Frequently the river rose to a point where the wheel had to be raised several feet above the bottom; fish then could escape below the sweep of the dips. To eliminate any loss of fish, it was therefore reasonable for inventive builders to devise means of forcing fish upward from the bottom into the path of the scoops. These attempts took the form of a movable false bottom, incline plane, or doors built into the dipway.

When debris piled up in front of the drift gate and could not be shoved aside, there was nothing to do but raise the wheel, lift the gate, and release the trash through the dipway. This was time consuming, and expensive if fish were running in abundance.

By observing where Indians were able to dipnet salmon, early fishwheel men determined their wheel sites. A number of these sites, especially in The Dalles-Celilo area, were in natural lava channels through which the current flowed at high-water periods. Others were blasted out of solid basalt. Indians had long known, and Caucasians soon learned, that salmon took momentary refuge in eddies downstream from rocky projections. Both scows and stationary wheels were placed at the upstream edge of an eddy where fish entered the main current again.

Another excellent site was near a submerged reef which caused the river to boil toward the surface; this vertical rising current also carried fish upward into the sweep of the wheel dips. Men painstakingly searched the "Narrows" of the Columbia for these upwellings.

Columbia River fishermen are well aware of net selectivity, in that the mesh size permits the escape of smaller fish, but these same men were puzzled when asked whether the fishwheels captured only the larger fish. Early wheel men knew that some machines caught more of one kind of fish than others, but they believed that different species and sizes of fish had different routes. Some thought that chinook would run deeper, and that blueback and steelhead would go into shallow water when given a choice.

Fishermen aver that blueback salmon actually do "talk," in an interpretive sense, by releasing bubbles of gas which reveal their migration paths. A person trained to the river can perceive the gas rising to the surface, deduce the presence of this smallest species of salmon, and discover likely wheel sites. While McNary Dam was being built, large numbers of these fish concentrated below the concrete structure, where the bubbles aided in locating them. This trait of expelling gas from their mouths and gills was also observed through the windows of the public fish-viewing room at John Day Dam during the summer of 1968. Except for occasionally leaping from the fishways, blueback do not ordinarily jump free of the water, but break surface with their tails and slap the air-water surface in a distinctive manner. This action is frequently noted in the downstream entrance to the Bonneville navigation lock adjacent to the swift current issuing from the powerhouse.

The salmon did not run so well when an east wind was blowing, when a sudden shower occurred, or in muddy, rapidly rising water. Bill Sams believed that, as a rule, the Cascade wheels caught more fish at night, though the largest catch ever made by his father's scow wheel was in the afternoon. He tended the wheel on the upper end of Ives Island and rowed home across the river about noon each day, coming back before dark. On one late June day there were chinook, steelhead, blueback, jacks, suckers, and "eels" all over the place. The next morning 2,500 pounds of salmon were shipped.

To Eric Enquist the night-time catches depended on the seasons. In general, the period from 4 a.m. until 8 a.m. brought the greatest abundance of salmon to his dips. As river flow diminishes throughout the summer, turbidity also decreases. The salmon could then see the lead and dips and evade them in the daytime, but at night when the fish could not see so well, apparently more were caught.

Alfred Hendricks worked 21 years on Warren wheels 16 and 19 at the Cascades, Washington. Wheel 19 was located below the rapids, while No. 16 was above them, at a point where the water began its rush down the falls. To reach Wheel 16, the fish had to ascend through the swift, turbulent water. Hendricks recalled heavy catches at night, particularly of blueback, thus proving salmon did travel over the rapids in darkness, though near the shore where the current was not so swift. When blueback are abundant, following the spring freshet as water flow and turbidity are diminishing, fish counters at the Columbia River dams have noted great numbers of this species still moving after dark.

Fewer sturgeon were taken above the rapids than below. Only a few sturgeon per year (a maximum of 27) ascend the Bonneville, Dalles, McNary, and other fishladders. These fish will, however, enter the Bonneville fishlocks readily, especially at night during late August and September.

Older river and wheel men, as well as biologists, have learned that salmon moving upstream against the current of a swiftly flowing river tend to follow shorelines, where irregularities of the banks and bottom reduce water velocity. Wheels were truly successful only in swift-water reaches of the stream where fish crowded close to the banks or ascended distinct channels leading directly to the revolving scoops, and where adequate current existed to turn the dippers briskly enough to entrap the wary migrants. Bluebacks follow such routes more closely than other salmon.

Night operators were not provided for the wheels. In the evening, before retiring, the regular tender anticipated the morning river levels and set the axle elevation accordingly. An especially conscientious or wakeful individual might check the wheel once or twice during the night, but this was exceptional. Of course, if any noise occurred, its source might be investigated, but as mentioned earlier, any difficulty usually awaited the morning hours.

FRANK REED OF CORBETT

Frank Reed, of Corbett, on the Lower River, was alone in believing that wheels and traps were most productive in clear water and daytime hours, when salmon could see the leads, be properly deflected by them, and guided into the dipway. To him, steelhead were easier to catch because they led better. A tape-recorded interview with Reed, age 85, was made on August 3, 1960, a few months before his death. He stated that the majority of fishwheels in the Corbett region were constructed by pioneer W. H. Reed and his five sons.

Numerous crayfish were noted in the Reed wheels. Other species caught besides salmon and steelhead were squawfish, sturgeon, bass, shad, lampreys, carp, sea-run cutthroat, suckers, a rare sculpin, chubs, trout, and whitefish. One year when a vast run of lampreys surged upstream, his men were compelled to use over-size pitchforks to remove "eels" from the fish box to make room for salmon. Apparently their number gave Reed the idea to profit from this resource by starting what he called an "eel oil factory." The "rendering plant" was only a huge iron kettle over a fire to "try" the fat from the lampreys. Reed recalled:

"The eels were good for oil, but it took the paint off the boats. . . . We captured them by the ton." Reed also used salmon heads from the Rooster Rock Cannery. The venture, though, failed because of lack of raw material from which to extract oil.

The Rooster Rock Cannery, built by the Columbia River Packers Association about 1880, faced the lagoon just west of Rooster Rock. At first, salmon delivery boats could bring fish directly to the building but successive freshets filled the bay with silt; whereupon piling was driven to make a trestle 12 feet wide upon which a tramway ran from the outer end to haul the fish. This arrangement continued for a few seasons, but the cost of the addi-

tional fish-handling necessitated moving the establishment to Ellsworth, Washington, about 1915. A photo taken by C. E. Watkins, in 1867, shows the area immediately downstream from Rooster Rock to be covered with sand. Later the sand washed away, leaving the lagoon or bay which provided such an excellent boat approach for the CRPA Cannery. Various photos taken over a period of many decades show that the sand filled and departed from the lagoon several times. Frank Reed recalled:

"I built a stationary wheel at Rooster Rock. The piling still stands there on the river side of the rock (1960). The dippers were about 15 feet wide and dipped perhaps 10 feet deep. The machine was larger than one we built at Onion Rock, but smaller than our Tunnel Point Wheel. We built all three right after the 1894 flood at around the same cost for each one, and it took a year apiece to build them."

Three other Reed stationary wheels were placed at 1-mile intervals on the Washington shore, in the vicinity of Mt. Pleasant: one slightly east of the store, another half a mile east of the Mt. Pleasant dock (this one caught more blueback), and the third at "old" Mt. Pleasant, about a mile downstream from the old dock. All were constructed after 1894 and completed before 1907; each had horizontal bar leads approximately 75 feet long.

The Reeds retained ownership of the Corbett Landing Wheel until the scarcity of salmon made operation and maintenance unprofitable. After severe damage in 1910 or 1911, the wheel finally washed out about 1916, lodging near Taylor siding. Only a few piling remain to show a wheel had once turned here.

"For pretty good money" the Reeds eventually sold their other wheels to the Columbia River Packers Association and Patrick McGowan. In fact, several of them were fabricated for the express purpose of sale to the larger outfits.

Frank Reed was among those who verified a pre-1900 floating wheel near the upper end of the Oregon Channel between Government Island and the mainland—the westernmost wheel on record on the river. The story is that Pete Antonsen, a "barefooted Dane" from sailship days, built a flimsy scow dipper here. Large bolts anchored in the Government Island sandstone secured the frail rotating structure, thrown together in crude fashion similar to the Indian scows of the Celilo region. Paddles to rotate the dips were made of 2x8 planks, and fish were directed into the scoops by a short, vertical picket lead driven diagonally from the rock bluff. The wheel took some blueback but was unprofitable. Antonsen sold it to Henry Stenson, who moved it several hundred feet downstream, where he fashioned another "Siwash" picket fence from old boards and other scraps. The new site was equally un-

successful, and the machine fell into ruin, or was washed away years before the fishwheel closure in 1926.

H. R. Reed (no kin of the Corbett Reeds) built a stationary installation late in 1906 and early 1907 on the channel end of the outboard lead built by the elder Sams for his No. 2 Wheel. Reed also erected a short riverside extension fence to shunt fish to the dipway, but his outer machine was not set right with the current, and as the river rose, the altered direction of water flow and increased velocities caused the wheel to shift to one side and jam.

Because the outer dipper did not function well, he tore it down in about two years, but not before a great amount of rock from Fisher's Quarry had been dumped there in an effort to stabilize the structure. He was censured for this venture, especially since he had been warned against it, but he was astute enough to entrust the remaining installation later to Eric Enquist who "turned" a profit.

Tunnel Wheel at Corbett. (Clifford Reed)

Fish Wheel, Columbia River, Oregon.

Looking downstream into dipway of what is believed to be one of the flimsy fishwheels near Mt. Pleasant and Lawton Creek on the Washington shore. Postcard from which picture was copied bore postmark, August 30, 1909. (George B. Abdill)

The Mt. Pleasant, Washington, stationary about 1900. (Thelma Ross Collection)

*Rooster Rock Cannery before silt deposits caused removal to Ellsworth, Washington.
(Gertrude Glutsch Jensen)*

Rooster Rock Cannery and tramway across sandspit.

Dr. Ferdinand Candiani, noted Columbia Gorge doctor. Pioneers recall his distillery and fishwheel at Distillery Point above Cape Horn. He later became Italian Consul in Portland.

George Breslin Landing at Cape Horn about 1909. S. P. & S. Railroad is on right. (Mrs. Clifford M. Ritter)

COLUMBIA GORGE—"THE RAINY BELT"

The "glory days" of fishwheels on the Columbia, however, were lived not on the Lower River, but on the upper—in the Cascades and The Dalles-Celilo areas, two radically different ecological regions which created distinctly different wheel maintenance problems. At the Cascades there was no respite for the constant wetness and rotting temperatures common during the entire year. Here, the sodden Pacific clouds drive inland and spill their 69 to 102 inches of rain each season. Wheels located in this rainy belt were supported by rock-filled cribs or driven piling, and the timbers above water level were soon destroyed by termites plus fungi.

In addition, the scorching winds of summer funneling down the Gorge split and wracked the structural timbers resting above water. Floating wheels beached on the sandy or rocky shores soon decayed to dust. Upkeep in the Cascades was a constant battle, with complete renovation necessary every few years. Apparently no wood preservative was used in the area.

Scows required more care than stationary wheels. Each year after the blueback run was over—about the middle of July—many wheels were beached. In the dry heat, joints would open widely, necessitating re-caulking before the next spring. The Sams brothers, Bill and Fred, have described how the leaky scows were put on sizable blocks of wood high enough for a repairman to crawl under the craft, and with a special tarbox and roller, replace oakum and tar in the seams. A wooden box approximately 6 inches wide, 12 inches long, and 6 inches deep, held the hot tar. A cross-rod served as axle for a wooden wheel with a groove in the perimeter. As this roller was trundled forward along the caulked seams in the bottom of the scow, the recess in its perimeter carried the melted tar from the supply in the box upward into the oakum, to achieve a better seal.

The Olympian *moored at Warren's Cannery, Warrendale, looking upstream. This must have been taken prior to construction of Sams' No. 1 (Rockcrusher Wheel) at point above the cannery. (Gertrude Glutsch Jensen)*

Winter view showing (1) Ira Dodson's upper wheel, (2) Warren Packing Company Cannery, (3) Myron B. Kelly fishwheel lead, and (4) Mosquito Island. Cabin was owned by William Ladzic and Rudolph Koch, fishermen. Photo was copyrighted in 1903 by the Kiser Brothers, who were introduced to photography when William Sargent Ladd commissioned Pearl White to ascend the river in a houseboat, the Pyrocraft, *to photograph river scenes. The Kiser family was living on the Columbia beach ranch near Dodson, Oregon, where Miss White stopped for a time.*

Another serious hazard in the Cascades for the wooden and less durable substructures was the ice jams in winter, which were especially bad below Bonneville. When a great block of ice broke loose, it tore out leads and sometimes wheels. Especially on the Oregon side, wheels were subject to damage from moving ice. Eric Enquist remembered one bad pile-up in 1915 when ice completely blocked the river below Garrison Rapids. He could feel the mass of ice start to shift after dark one evening in January, and hear the piling of the fishwheels cracking and breaking.

"It was a long night for me to wait to learn whether my investment was wiped out," Enquist said, "but only the voters later succeeded in causing the loss of my $50,000 enterprise." As mentioned earlier, Oregon outlawed the wheels in 1926.

In sharp contrast to the Cascades region, The Dalles-Celilo area was hotter and drier than "the hinges of Hades" in the summer; very little rain fell to give fungi or rot a chance to destroy the wooden portions of the wheels. Although the searing heat and dry winds laden with "blow sand" caused the timbers to split, deterioration was slow. The few fall and spring rains of the wheel epoch were not enough to cause damage.

The Tahoma *trapped in ice floe opposite Archer Mountain, January 6-February 12, 1916. Still trapped in an ice floe, it broke loose and crushed the Reed Tunnel Point Wheel. (Hans Blaser)*

Frozen Columbia River about 1907. P. J. McGowan's fishwheel gins show at right through the trees with Cascade Navigation Locks beyond. (Dorothy P. Nile)

PART TWO

THE DALLES-CELILO REGION

Frank Seufert in younger years.
(Edra Ann Dielschneider)

Early Phelps Wheel before reconstruction with concrete base. It made its greatest catches during the flood of 1894.

FRANK A. SEUFERT

Fishwheels on both shores of the Columbia River in The Dalles-Celilo area extended from below Chenoweth Creek west of The Dalles upstream to Celilo Falls—probably the greatest Indian salmon fishing grounds in the world. Beginning as early as 1883 or 1884, these dippers were owned and used by many individuals and companies, but the major operator was Seufert Brothers Company, pioneer salmon and fruit packer of The Dalles. The company held deeds to land containing fishing rights on both sides of the river. These lands were purchased at different times from a number of private owners as well as from the State of Oregon. At one time the company operated 19 stationary wheels, 17 scows, and 4 seines.

Founder of the company, Frank A. Seufert, was born in Long Island, New York, in 1853. With five dollars in his pocket, he arrived alone in San Francisco in the mid-1870s, seeking his fortune. After marriage and the birth of his first son, Arthur, he left San Francisco in 1881 with his family, bound for Walla Walla, Washington Territory. However, upon witnessing the booming business activity in The Dalles—a transfer point for river steamers and inland freight wagons—he decided to stop there.

That same year with $600 in savings, Seufert launched a small business on the north side of Second Street between Court and Union, buying and selling fresh fruit, poultry, meat, and fish. It was here that he became acquainted with Columbia River salmon when Indians brought their fish to his place of business. Frank Seufert was soon joined by his younger brother, Theodore, and together they organized the firm called Seufert Brothers.

In 1883, the Oregon Railway and Navigation Company established a flag station immediately west of Fifteenmile Creek Crossing, naming it "Seufert." (This was changed to "Seuferts" in 1896, and has so remained.) The following year the brothers purchased the land at the station and also started one of the first large irrigated orchards in Eastern Oregon. In 1885, they built their first fishwheel, and by 1890, had constructed five more dippers between Seuferts and Celilo, having acquired the land.

The total number of stationary fishing machines in The Dalles-Celilo area was 34, with Seufert Brothers Company having been responsible for building, leasing, or purchasing 19 of them.

On September 2, 1892, Seufert Brothers Company bought the Mitchell Fishery from William Mitchell and Company, the property including an ice house, salmon saltery, and the Phelps Wheel, on land lying a few hundred yards east of the present bridge at The Dalles. Phelps had farmed the land before selling it to Mitchell, who then erected the revolving dipper. The purchase proved most propitious two years later, in 1894.

On May 27, 1894, the Columbia River, rising toward its highest recorded stage in history, destroyed or damaged all the Seufert wheels except the Phelps, which was built to fish in very high water. Stationary dippers owned by other wheel men were also lost. The river continued to rise until it peaked on June 6, flooding First, Second, and even part of Third Street in The Dalles, with the brewery on Third remaining the only "dry" spot. Townspeople fortunately could drown their sorrows in beer instead of river water. On the window casement (approximately 4⅔ feet above the sidewalk) at Weigelt Bros., a book and stationery store in The Dalles, is a marker showing the extreme elevation of the 1894 flood, which is far above the normal pool elevation at Bonneville.

In June and July, 1894, the Phelps Wheel made its largest catches, taking 226,870 pounds of salmon between May 17 and July 31, and peaking at 42,360 pounds (mostly blueback) on July 2. It never again succeeded in catching even one-fifth this number in a single season. But as a result of its one phenomenal success, the Phelps dipper paid for the repair of all the remaining Seufert wheels damaged by the flood.

In later years, some unsuccessful innovations were made in attempts to improve its fish-catching ability. The dippers were widened to a breadth greater than the channel immediately below, a pothole was dug to enable the dipping buckets to reach deeper and possibly prevent salmon from swimming beneath the wheel, and the channel was deepened 6 feet at the mouth—but all to no avail. Following this one spectacular season, yearly catches averaged 2 to 8 tons. Until reduced to ashes on June 5, 1963, the Phelps structure (minus dippers) was the last salmon wheel to stand on the Columbia River. It could be seen on the Oregon shore a short distance upstream from The Dalles Bridge.

By 1896, the Seufert brothers were well established in the cannery business. Their plant at Seuferts Station was capable of turning out 1,000 cases of one-pound flats per day, equivalent to 32 tons of salmon. Actually, during large salmon runs, between 1,000 and 1,200 cases were processed daily by extending the work day. The boilers were fired by 4-foot slabwood, with two cords of wood required daily.

Seufert Brothers Company built their first stationary fishwheel on the Columbia opposite the present powerhouse of The Dalles Dam and called it No. 1. This was the only Seufert wheel on which a fatality occurred; a collapsing beam killed one of the workers during construction. No. 1 was destroyed by the 1894 flood and rebuilt the following winter, but was finally abandoned after the 1914 fishing season. The best year for this wheel was 1909 when 40,186 pounds were taken. It caught only 498 pounds in

1894 before the flood, and in some years averaged around 8 tons, but in each of its last 5 seasons of operation, it averaged only about 3½ tons of fish.

No. 2 was located just downstream from the mouth of Fifteenmile Creek. Like No. 1, it, too, was destroyed by the 1894 flood. However, it was not rebuilt until the winter of 1912-13, resuming operation the following spring. In 1922 the wooden cribbing was replaced by a new dipway of concrete, which can still be seen outlining the fishwheel channel.

Like all the stationary wheels located downstream from Celilo, No. 2 was built to fish in relatively high water for spring chinook and blueback. Water stages in the fall were much too low for operation. In 1948, Hank Wickman, long-time employee who operated Seufert boats and scow wheels between Big Eddy and Celilo, burned the wheel to improve accessibility to the channel for dipnetting operations. Although it caught both large and small salmon, No. 2's largest seasonal catch was 15,968 pounds in 1922, with the average each year being about 5 tons.

Seufert's Wheel No. 1, originally built in 1885 and rebuilt in the form seen here following the 1894 flood. This was the first fishwheel built by Frank A. Seufert, founder of the company. Photograph was taken during lower water period in 1901 by Arthur Seufert. (Oregon Historical Society)

Western terminus of The Dalles-Celilo Portage Railroad about 1910. (Oregon Historical Society)

The Dalles-Celilo Portage Railroad, 1867, by C. E. Watkins, pioneer photographer. Note how the blowsand has drifted. (Oregon Historical Society)

Construction of The Dalles-Celilo Canal, looking west toward Big Eddy and lower end of the canal. This photo was taken December 5, 1913, during low water. (Oregon Historical Society)

Upper end of The Dalles-Celilo Canal. Tumwater fishwheel at lower left and Taffe fishwheels at upper right are visible. (Oregon Historical Society)

Seufert's No. 2 fishwheel, built in winter of 1885-86. Seufert scow is to the right of No. 2, with the mouth of Fifteenmile Creek, at left, and Chinese bunkhouse on top of ledge. (Edra Ann Dielschneider)

Seufert's No. 2 wheel after concrete dipway was constructed. (Oregon Historical Society)

While not the best wheel in this area, No. 3—built by Seufert in 1886—was rated just a notch below the top producers. The best year was 1922 when 77,040 pounds, about 38 tons, were taken. Catches ranged down to less than 2 tons in 1915, and averaged about 16 tons per season throughout the working life of the wheel. The wheel caught blueback and large chinook salmon, primarily.

No. 4 Wheel, built the same year, 1886, was constructed on a high-water course lying between the river channel and the regular south bank, upstream from No. 3, near what was called "The Fishery"—a term derived from the old Whitcomb Fishery situated on the Oregon shore a mile or so upstream from Big Eddy. No. 4 caught large salmon and blueback,

its daily timing of catches coinciding with that of No. 3. Its peak season was in 1910 when it caught 46,105 pounds, but many years, only 2 to 4 tons were caught. Its lifetime average was about 7 tons per season.

No. 4 was also destroyed by the 1894 flood but was rebuilt that fall. On November 6, 1956, the cribbing and superstructure were burned in reservoir-clearing operations prior to raising The Dalles pool. The only wheel parts saved were the axle and flanges. At that time it was planned to rebuild the old wheel and place it on display at a park to be located at the Seufert Cannery, but the park did not materialize and the wheel parts remain in the old cannery building, gathering cobwebs.

Looking upstream toward fishwheel No. 3, originally built by Seufert in 1886, and rebuilt following 1894 flood. Dry fishwheel channel shows in foreground (low water). Photo was taken by Arthur Seufert in 1901. (Oregon Historical Society)

The Georgie Burton *pushing barge, with No. 4 Seufert fishwheel in foreground, during high water. (Edra Ann Dielschneider)*

THOSE SENSITIVE SALMON

Fish were not the only migrants in the upper waters. C. W. Cleland of The Dalles told of an incident wherein Seuferts' No. 4 wheel had been catching an abundance of fish during a spring run in 1908, when suddenly its productivity stopped, while another wheel fairly close by but in another channel was still doing well. Upon investigating, Cleland said he found a dead cow above No. 4. About an hour after the cow had been dislodged, the wheel again caught salmon.

Especially in the channels and eddies below Nos. 3 and 4, seals occasionally appeared and frightened the fish. Operators were supplied with a gun and told to kill or drive away the animals whenever they appeared. One of the old 44-caliber Winchester carbines used for this purpose is still in possession of Francis Seufert at The Dalles.

According to the 1888 Report of the Oregon State Board of Fish Commissioners: "Hundreds of seals can be seen in the month of July at The Dalles, 200 miles distant from the mouth of the river, and it has been estimated that one seal will eat or destroy 8 to 10 full-size salmon in 24 hours."

An Indian dipnetter above The Dalles Bridge in 1959 correctly attributed the departure of salmon from his netting area to the presence of a human corpse in the water. Search in adjacent driftwood disclosed the body. One of the authors in recent years saw a costly research experiment ruined by human odor. The study was progressing beautifully, with hundreds of fish streaming up the narrow experimental fish ladder when the bare toes of a researcher accidentally touched the water; the rush of fish stopped instantly.

It is interesting that almost all fishwheels did not catch well during their first season of operation. It was thought the smell of fresh concrete in the cribbing caused fish to avoid the adjacent waters. Freshly creosoted timbers, used in rock-filled cribbing, also reputedly caused salmon to reject the area. On one occasion, Frank Seufert ordered a newly built cribbing of creosoted timbers removed, after lack of success in initial operation of the Cyclone Wheel was attributed to the creosote odor.

No. 5 fishwheel, originally built in winter of 1886-87, was rebuilt immediately following 1894 flood in the form seen here. The best fishwheel on this reach of the river, it established a record seasonal catch of salmon (209 tons in 1906) and a record daily catch (35 tons on May 10, 1913). Seufert Brothers established a warehouse here (at head of Fivemile Rapids) and called the area Tenino. (Oregon Historical Society)

View from Oregon shore looking downstream toward No. 5 fishwheel located at head of Fivemile Rapids, about 1900. Scow fishwheel upstream from No. 5 can be seen operating at left. Note boards placed across part of flow in attempt to divert upstream moving fish to scow wheel. (Oregon Historical Society)

FAMOUS NO. 5

The most famous salmon wheel of all, No. 5, caught more fish and made more money than any fishwheel on the Columbia River, and probably in the world—and it was the focal point of contention during the many years of perennial fish fights between Seufert Brothers Company and the fishermen of the lower Columbia. No. 5 caught 417,855 pounds of salmon in 1906, about 209 tons, the largest amount taken in a single season by any wheel in this area. Its greatest daily catch, a record for this section of the river, was 35 tons on May 10, 1913. It averaged approximately 73 tons per season during its lifetime; the lowest yearly catch was 10½ tons in 1926. In a statement of fixed company assets dated October 31, 1892, the cost of this premier dipper was listed as $8,890.97. In a misguided effort to make a fine thing better, the wheel channel entrance was deepened about 6 feet in the winter of 1919. This proved to be a mistake, as the water velocity at the entrance was reduced, and fewer salmon were attracted into the dipway channel.

Constructed in 1887, No. 5, along with many others, was badly damaged by the 1894 flood. Rebuilt in the fall of 1896, it continued producing until stopped by court order. Though the operation of fishwheels was outlawed by voters in the State of Oregon in 1926, Wheel No. 5 was used until stopped by court order, July 1, 1927. The wheel burned to the ground on October 24, 1956.

At No. 5's location near the head of Fivemile Rapids, Seufert also built a warehouse alongside the Oregon Railroad and Navigation Company's tracks and named it Tenino. Fivemile and Tenmile rapids on the Columbia were designated by the government engineers as being that distance from the boat landing at the City of The Dalles. This nomenclature followed the practice of naming Threemile, Fivemile, Eightmile, and Fifteenmile creeks in the 1850-1860 period.

Seufert next erected a fishwheel riverward from No. 4 in another but similar channel, during the winter of 1893-94. Because Wheels Nos. 4 and 5 were already constructed, he called the new one No. 4½. The name, however, was of little consequence because the 1894 flood destroyed the dipper and it was never rebuilt, thus giving No. 4½, along with Seufert's Washington Wheel across the river, the distinction of having one of the most abbreviated lives of all fishwheels in this area—an example of the risks in the gamble called fishing.

In the winter of 1895-1896, Seufert, seeking to prepare for another flood of the size of the 1894 one, built an adjacent wheel inside — shoreward — from No. 5 on a very high water channel; he called it No. 6. Not until the 1948 flood did the water level again rise sufficiently to turn the dippers of this wheel. However, though the dippers were raised and the wheel turned, it was not in true fishing position. Hans Blaser of The Dalles took motion pictures of it as it revolved in the flood waters. By this time, of course, the use of salmon wheels had long been prohibited on the Columbia.

Construction of this wheel to take advantage of another extremely high-river stage, like the one in 1894, was a long chance which never paid off. Cost of the "white elephant" was between $6,000 and $7,000—a huge sum in those days. The structure was burned on October 25, 1956, during clearing operations for The Dalles Dam.

"BIG NO. 1"

In contrast to other Seufert Wheels in The Dalles-Celilo area, Tumwater No. 1 and No. 2 were low-water wheels built primarily for fall fishing. Constructed in the winter of 1889-90, Tumwater No. 1 was located at Tumwater, a station on the O. R. & N. Railway opposite Celilo Falls, and had, in conjunction with it, a warehouse and fish house. Chris Kitto, a veteran Seufert employee who operated the Cyclone and Bay wheels in the spring, moved to Celilo in late summer and fall to operate Tumwater No. 1 and the fish house.

When first constructed, this wheel had a rock-filled timber cribbing; later this was changed to concrete. A long cableway extended from the machine across wild waters to Big Island (one of the Celilo group) for transporting Indian fishermen and the salmon they caught with spears and dipnets.

Tumwater No. 1 was one of the three best fish catchers in this part of the Columbia, and there was no wheel larger on the "upper river." Salmon were hauled by box cars on the O. R. & N. tracks from Tumwater Station to Seuferts Cannery. Old box cars, destined to be scrapped in Portland, were used, with each car limited to about 5 tons of salmon per trip. The thousands of people who visited Celilo every fall to watch Indians harvest the great salmon runs may remember this dipper—a huge, towering structure rising from the riverbank, landward from The Dalles-Celilo Canal and within easy view from U.S. Highway 30.

Tumwater No. 1 averaged about 38 tons of salmon per season, with its greatest catch (290,365 pounds) being made in 1923. The lowest yearly total was in 1899, with 10,220 pounds. The structure was burned on November 8, 1956 in the reservoir-clearing operations for The Dalles Dam.

The older version of Tumwater fishwheel at Celilo in foreground, with timber and rock-filled cribs. In middle background are three Taffe fishwheels, and the cannery at Celilo Falls. (Oregon Historical Society)

Tumwater fishwheel at left and Little Tumwater to the right, on Oregon shore at Celilo Falls. Indian dwellings can be seen in the foreground. Picture was taken before construction of The Dalles-Celilo Canal. (Oregon Historical Society)

PORTABLE WHEELS

Tumwater No. 2, or the "Little Tumwater," was a portable "take down" wheel first fished by Seufert in 1897, in a channel cutting through the rock just downstream from Tumwater No. 1, but at a much lower elevation. When the river had receded sufficiently, the dipper arms, together with all their components, were set in place and fixed to fish. After the fall run was over, the wheel was dismantled and the parts stored for another season. "Little Tumwater" was an excellent fishing machine, averaging slightly over 18 tons of salmon per year throughout its operating life, with its best yearly catch of 114,670 pounds being made in 1906. However, only 935 pounds were taken in 1908.

The Cement Wheel was also a portable, take-down affair, built by Seufert in the winter of 1905-1906, and so-called because all the cribbing and channel sides were constructed of concrete. Prior to use each year, the dippers and the rest of the equipment were placed on pushcarts and trundled along a narrow-gauge railroad track across the rocks

out to the site, and there assembled. At the close of the season, or when high water threatened, all parts were removed by the same route. The wheel channel was located on the south bank a short distance below the head of Fivemile Rapids. While a homely looking affair, the Cement Salmon Wheel was one of the three top producers in the area. Its peak season was in 1910 when it captured 154,940 pounds. This river-powered scoop averaged 32 tons per year; its lowest yearly catch was 7 tons in 1925.

Tumwater No. 3 was built by Seufert about 1896 on the Oregon shore of the river, a few hundred yards downstream from Tumwater No. 1. Its short existence was ended by ice in the winter of 1898. The wheel was not rebuilt because the other Tumwater wheels and the Celilo seines furnished enough fall fish for cannery requirements. In later years, the wheel cribbing could be seen a few hundred feet west of the Celilo Railroad Bridge and opposite the swinging bridge over The Dalles-Celilo Canal at that point.

Charles Rosentreter, an early fisherman, said that while working as an inspector on the S. P. & S. Railroad grade in 1907, he observed the bleached remains of a small "portable stationary" wheel half a mile east of the railroad tunnel, a short distance above Wishram, Washington. He reported that a fishway channel, in which the dipper rotated, had been cut through a point of rock extending into the river.

In 1923, Seufert Brothers Company built two portables to fish below the China Pete machine at Eightmile Rapids, near Dillon on the Oregon shore. These were known as Cramer No. 1 and No. 2, as they were across from the old Cramer Wheel site. The old Cramer Wheel catch was moderate; the highest yearly take was 23,280 pounds in 1913 and the average annual poundage captured was about 7 tons. This was originally a scow wheel site; Hill and Reese had operated there as early as 1897. A

few years later, Emerson and Burgraff purchased the scow from the earlier operators and built a stationary dipper at the same location, calling it the Emerson Wheel. Then, in 1909, Bill Cramer bought the machine.

The wheel continued to fish through the 1916 season. After suffering heavy damage from high water in 1916 and 1917, it was removed in the fall of the latter year. The story is told of a large sturgeon that once became jammed between the fish box and the chute leading from one of the dips of the old Cramer Wheel. After all other efforts failed to dislodge the huge fish, it was finally chopped in two, whereupon the dippers again resumed turning.

The other company units, known as the Osborn and Osborn-Cramer scows, also fished at one time in the area at the upper end of Rabbit (Brown's) Island and beyond.

Cement Wheel, built in the winter of 1905-06, was removed and replaced each season. In background are No. 5 and No. 6 fishwheels at head of Fivemile Rapids. (Oregon Historical Society)

The Upper China Pete Wheel prior to purchase by Seufert Brothers Company in 1907. (Oregon Historical Society)

The Upper China Pete Wheel is on the left, and the Cramer Wheel on the right. The latter was not reconstructed after severe damage in the 1916 spate. (Oregon Historical Society)

SEUFERT BROTHERS COMPANY

The largest spring salmon pack made by Seufert Brothers Company was 17,947 cases in 1909, with the greatest fall salmon output being 17,271 cases in 1941. That same year the company packed 28,431 cases, the most for a single season. Fancy grades of salmon were marketed under the label, "Annie's Favorite"; choice grades were labeled "Merrimac Brand," and standard grades, "Tenino Brand." A separate fruit and vegetable branch of the company handled cherries, peaches, apricots, prunes, and peas. Much of the fruit was produced by Seuferts' own orchards, although a considerable amount was purchased from local orchardists and vegetable growers, with the company paying cash on delivery—which system was naturally popular with the farmers. Distribution of the company's products, through brokers, was nation-wide, with the East and South being especially heavy buyers of canned salmon. In the company's early days, the great cattle ranches in Montana were important purchasers of fruits, and the names of their headquarters dot the old account books.

As part of the cannery establishment, the company kept a large entourage of house cats to control mice. The cats' diet was augmented, naturally enough, by a daily ration of canned salmon. Late each year, the cannery made a special run of the inferior grade, late-fall "tullies," canning 40 to 50 cases just for the felines. The company also had a ubiquitous, loud-talking raven which had been injured and nursed back to health. This bird was no respecter of womanhood, and many a lady visitor to the cannery suffered torn silk stockings from the beak of this raucous character. While always amused, Frank Seufert would offer his consolations and the money for a new pair of hose. Perhaps justly, the black rascal reached the end of his turbulent career with a well-aimed potshot from a .22 rifle.

Seuferts provided a bunkhouse and furnished meals for its single employees, as well as houses for the foremen and bookkeeper. "Headquarters" in town for all hands was Charlie Frank's famous Horn Saloon, which contained one of the finest collections of firearms and stuffed wild animals and antlered and horned trophies ever brought together in one place. Unfortunately, the emporium, together with its invaluable collection, burned the evening of April 15, 1942.

The Seuferts always used Chinese crews in their cannery operations. All dealings between the management and the Chinese were made with and through the Chinese foreman, and in all the company's years of operation the Chinese crew had only six overseers: Seid Seid, Seid Kee, Seid Dai, Seid Fong, Seid Sing, all of the same family, and Yee Gum, the last of the company's Chinese "crew pushers." Since all the foremen had been salmon butchers at one time, they were called "Butch." Chinese butchers could clean a salmon in 45 seconds, which meant removal of the head, tail, fins, and viscera. It was often said that, in their hands, these Chinese workmen combined the strength of a man and the dexterity of a woman.

The Orientals were hired for six months and were paid a flat fee for the entire period regardless of the amount of salmon canned in the season. Since they were hired in Portland, the company also paid their round-trip fare from and to that city. This crew consisted of 45 to 50 men, including a Chinese cook and bookkeeper. Groceries and quarters for the entire group were furnished by Seuferts. The quarters consisted of a bunk house. Also provided was a hog pen with several swine. The Orientals kept the pen scrupulously clean with daily scrubbings. Supplies were purchased from a Chinese grocer in Portland and sent to the cannery periodically by train.

No Chinese crew would begin work on a Friday, for they believed beginning a new salmon season that day would bring only bad luck to everyone. In deference to this superstition, the company never started their Chinese crews on a Friday, because, after all, these men could have been right!

TUGS and TENDERS

Frank Seufert's interests were diversified. His company also owned and operated five gasoline-powered tugs and salmon tenders. The *Lillie* was a wooden-hulled craft built about 1910 and abandoned in the early twenties, after being used to serve the company's scow wheels in The Dalles and Big Eddy areas. The *Hyack*, also wooden-hulled, and built in the early twenties at St. Helens, was considered among the best fast-water salmon tenders ever built, but was abandoned after fishwheels were outlawed.

The *Hyack* was brought from St. Helens to The Dalles by the renowned river pilot, Captain Stewart V. Winslow. According to local history, in 1904, when the captain was a young man, he put together a home-made airplane mounted on a bicycle. While furiously pedaling down the steep hayfield behind Seuferts Cannery, in a determined attempt to launch his contraption into the air, his dreams of becoming an aerial pioneer came to a sudden and disastrous end; an unexpected obstacle in his path launched him, instead, right in the middle of a haystack. Local history records no further such experiments.

The Seufert *Chinook* was similar to the *Hyack*, serving for years as a salmon pick-up boat. Being fast and handling extremely well in surging water, she was especially adapted for working below the railroad bridge at Celilo. When oarsmen for the seine boats were difficult to locate and employ, the *Chinook* towed the seining craft while nets were set below the falls. She was abandoned in 1953. The *Steelhead* was a steel-hulled pick-up boat built in Portland during World War I. This vessel was slow but possessed a large carrying capacity, and was used at Celilo Landing during the fall chinook run.

Immediately following World War II, Seuferts—whose activities included seining—used an Army DUKW, the *Silverside*, to lay out their seines at Oregon Bar No. 1 below Celilo. This was the first and probably the only DUKW used in a Columbia River seining operation. In 1954, the *Silverside* was sold to a businessman of The Dalles, after which it successively appeared as a transporter of live salmon by Washington State Department of Fisheries in their research study at McNary Dam; as a work boat in early construction phases at the Ice Harbor Dam project on the Snake River; and then—when her balky engine and leaky hull forced her into retirement from the river—as a parade float in Walla Walla, Washington, wrapped in bunting and carrying pretty girls. When last seen, she was forlornly rusting in an Eastern Washington junkyard.

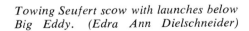

Towing Seufert scow with launches below Big Eddy. (Edra Ann Dielschneider)

97

Seuferts seined below Celilo Falls at Oregon Bar No. 1, Oregon Bar No. 2, Washington Bar No. 2, and Clanton's Bar. The goal each day was to lay out and haul a seine once each daylight hour, thus making a long, hard day for both men and horses. Below Celilo Falls the salmon ran abundantly at daybreak, with the first seine haul in the morning often being the best one of the day. As the sun rose higher, each successive sweep caught fewer fish. However, when sundown approached, the catches improved and the last haul in the evening sometimes equalled the first attempt at dawn. The largest catch from Washington seine Bar No. 2 was 236 tons in 1897, with the Oregon Bar No. 1 seine capturing 239 tons in 1948. The latter net provided the largest daily catch ever made by a company seine—35 tons on September 13, 1947. Seines were prohibited by Oregon voters in 1948, but under court injunction the practice continued until September 14, 1950.

All told, Frank Seufert enjoyed a distinct advantage over other wheel men by ownership of the greatest number of wheel sites and possession of the lands bordering the swiftest water on the river. He and his men suffered disaster from floods also, but

nevertheless managed to erect some of the strongest, most durable wheels ever built. And, only Seufert, and possibly William Sargent Ladd, the banker friend of Frank Warren, lived to enjoy the rewards of their industry. Wilson earned not a farthing from his idea. McCord, no businessman, was forced from his wheel at Bradford Island to an unproductive spot near Prindle, Washington. Frank Warren went down with the *Titanic* in 1912. William Sams, Sr., who broke the Warren Cascades monopoly, sold to the Columbia River Packers Association. Eric Enquist was defeated by the voters in 1926 and 1934, and lost his $50,000 investment.

Frank Seufert, though, became a millionaire, later moved to Portland, dying there on December 11, 1929 at the age of 76. Following his death, ownership and management of Seufert Brothers Company was assumed by his sons—Arthur, William, and Edward. In 1954, the Federal government purchased most of the company property for construction of The Dalles Lock and Dam by the U. S. Army Corps of Engineers. Seufert Brothers, established in 1881, had operated continuously for 73 years, all within the same family.

Seufert's seining operation near Wishram Bridge. (Edra Ann Dielschneider)

Seufert's seining operation below Celilo, probably at Washington Bar, showing No. 2 seine and running team of horses. (Edra Ann Dielschneider)

THE KLINDT WHEEL

In this upriver area, the westernmost wheel was probably that of Henry Klindt. Older residents of The Dalles still recall a "fleet" of scow wheels operating on the Columbia to the west of their city, and details of at least three stationaries definitely can be recalled. Forgotten wheels may have been tested in the 40 or more miles of slowly moving water between Cascade Locks and Wascopam (The Dalles); but there is no precise knowledge of them—and there is of the Klindt Wheel.

In 1896, Walter Klindt's father, a pioneer stone mason of The Dalles, raised the Klindt Wheel on the Oregon shore at the point of rocks just downstream from, and adjacent to, the mouth of Chenoweth Creek. Anchor rods were cemented into the basalt rimrock to secure it to the shore. A vertical adjustment of about 8 feet was provided by means of 4 inside and 4 outside 12x12-inch upright timbers 60 feet long, tied into a framework by numerous crosspieces. An inside crib gave stability, but there

was no outside cribbing. However, a 10-foot wing, projecting riverward from the outer wall of the dipway, was designed to lead fish to the dippers.

During high water the dips turned about two revolutions per minute, but when the spring freshet subsided, the wheel would barely revolve in the sluggish current. For 20 years the Klindts walked a mile or so to the wheel once daily to remove only two or three fish each time, or none at all. Exceptional days did occur at the peak of the runs (particularly blueback), and the wheel would capture "several hundred pounds" of salmon each day for two or three days. But with a lifetime of fishing experience as a basis for review, Walter Klindt stated flatly: "That wheel was a total failure. The trouble was, the fish runs were diminishing and the fish remaining had too much room to go by the wheels." For this reason, fishermen in that area reverted to the use of nets.

By 1916 the wheel had deteriorated, and rather than reconstruct, Klindt permitted some of his relatives to salvage the 60-foot timbers for building a bridge. In dismantling the wheel, the 4-inch steel axle and flanges slipped from the rigging into the deep water, where scuba divers may possibly find the assembly if they choose to try.

Klindt was also a sturgeon fisherman; his best catch was 10 sturgeon on one line, each averaging about 200 pounds. The largest he ever caught topped the scales at approximately 600 pounds. Once as a youth, while pulling a sturgeon into his boat during the winter, he slipped on the ice and fell on a sturgeon hook, driving it into his knee. A fisherman by the name of Bob Rooney, camped near Crates Point west of The Dalles, came to his rescue, retrieved the sturgeon, carried Klindt ashore, and then sent for Dr. Logan, who removed the hook. Rooney later caught an 1100-pound sturgeon, the largest Klindt had ever seen.

Nine-hundred-pound sturgeon caught at The Dalles, Oregon. The Indian boy's right hand rests on the pectoral fin. Cross-sections of the anterior (front) ray of this fin are examined to determine the age of the fish.

OTHER STATIONARY WHEELS

Upriver from the Klindt Wheel, a few iron bars projecting over the river from the rimrock near The Dalles Mixing Plant are all that is left of the effort of Harry Lansdale and Bill Moody to reap the bounty of the river. Their stationary wheel was 30 to 36 feet in diameter and 8 feet wide, with the same type cribbing as the Klindt and Brown wheels. Very deep water could be found a few feet out from the structure. A fair current existed during average river flows to turn the dips, but at low water they would barely move. Evidence is conflicting as to the year this fishing machine was constructed. Some say it was prior to the 1894 flood, while others contend it was shortly afterward, with the later date probably more accurate. At any rate, this wheel caught only enough fish to pay for the annual license. It gradually fell into disrepair and was not used after 1905.

Hawaiian Louis Brown erected a third stationary rotary fishing machine below The Dalles in 1895 or 1896, about the same time as the Lansdale-Moody venture. The Brown or "Kanaka" scoop was slightly smaller than the other though, being only 24 to 26 feet in diameter and possibly 6 feet wide. The customary iron rods deeply imbedded in the rimrock, plus an inboard crib, held it to the cliff side. A short wing may have guided a few errant salmon into the dipway. It was considered a fairly good chinook wheel when first installed but conditions changed. Although Brown apparently retained ownership until it grew unprofitable, it eventually "just disappeared." Brown later married an Indian girl and moved to the Yakima area.

None of these three stationary wheels—the Klindt, the Lansdale-Moody, and the Brown—caught fall chinook, since lower flows in the Columbia at that season had insufficient velocity to turn the dippers.

"Old Julick," a carpenter and "squaw man," and his partner, a Mr. Lauer, selected as the site for their fishwheel a high-water channel several hundred feet west of the present site of The Dalles bridge. Constructed in 1896, it was a medium-size machine of average production and usable only in high water. Fish were hauled to the Seufert Cannery in a wagon. The dippers fell into disrepair and the wheel was eventually abandoned.

Old Julick. (Edra Ann Dielschneider)

101

Julick was very fond of Frank Seufert, Jr., and when the old "squaw man" died, he left his possessions—including an excellent set of carpenter and pipefitter tools and what was believed to be a sack of metal washers—to Frank. Apparently Frank never examined the contents before succumbing to the influenza epidemic of 1918, and the implement kit remained unopened and unused in the cannery basement.

In the early 1920s, when pipes froze in the Seufert residence on Fourth Street in The Dalles, Frank, Sr., sent Chris Peterson and Hank Wickman to thaw and otherwise repair the pipes. Wickman opened the old tool box, carelessly tossed a sack of washers aside, and selected the tools he needed. When the task was finished, he returned the sack of washers to the tool chest. The chest remained in The Dalles for four or five years, then was moved back to the cannery attic for two or three years more. One day Guy Whipple, while searching through the chest for a carpenter's plane, opened the "bag of washers" and what he saw sent him rushing to the office. Frank Seufert took a quick look, then called Chris Peterson.

"Chris, have you seen this bag before?"

"Yes."

"Did you know what was in it?"

"No," Chris replied.

"Here, Whipple," Frank said, "empty the bag into Chris's hands."

Twenty-nine Double Eagle gold pieces cascaded from the bag and overflowed Guy Whipple's cupped palms.

Old Julick once owned all the shacks now standing on the river bank just east of The Dalles Bridge, including the old Shaker church. When he died in 1915, his widow returned to the reservation at Simnasho.

Julick's wheels at The Dalles. (Mrs. Ed Seufert)

SCOWS FOLLOW FLOOD

The Rorick salmon wheels were built by T. J. Rorick in 1896 at the bend of Threemile Rapids on the Washington shore. They were not outstanding salmon catchers—averaging less than 4 or 5 tons per year—but they were considered adept at catching sturgeon. These wheels were eventually torn down and scow wheels fished in their place.

In the opinion of those familiar with scow wheels, the first ones appeared immediately after the 1894 flood. As a result of the damage to nearly all the stationary wheels by that high water, scows were built and fished at many of the old, washed-out dipper locations. Realizing the damage another flood of similar magnitude could do to fixed installations, some operators changed to floating wheels exclusively. Scows were not restricted to certain "choice" locations as were stationary wheels, and their mobility afforded the owners a chance to try their luck at different spots. And, because they were less expensive than the fixed wheels, more fishermen could try their luck with them.

Near the turn of the century, "Old Man Davis" operated a scow a few hundred yards below Walter Klindt's boat harbor. If anything went amiss, he was close by to make corrections, for he lived in a one-room shack on the fishing craft. It was a conventional, improved-type scow wheel, with the dips rotating between two timber shafts projecting downstream over the stern of the floating support. A bare existence rewarded this venture, and following 3 or 4 years of trial, it "just disappeared," along with Davis.

Henry Lauritson, in early partnership with Andrew Hansen, constructed three scow wheels in 1897, locating them on the Washington shore below The Dalles and opposite Walter Klindt's home. These machines had wooden cribbings built outside the 24-foot diameter dippers, which may have aided in diverting a few fish to the revolving dips. However, the venture was abandoned as a failure in a few years. Around 1896, Caleb Hill constructed and operated a portable wheel on the Washington shore about a mile above those owned by Henry Lauritson. After a few seasons, this endeavor also grew to be "not worth the candle," and the craft disappeared.

As with the stationary salmon wheels, some scows caught many more salmon than others. The two best that fished in The Dalles-Celilo region were the Bluejay Scow and the Grass Island No. 1, both on the Washington side. The Grass Island made the largest daily catch of any scow in this area with 10,838 pounds of spring salmon taken on May 8, 1933, and the largest seasonal catch in the same year—a total of 90,054 pounds.

The Grass Island Scow Wheels Nos. 1 and 2, the Bluejay, the Rorick, and the Joe Esterbrook scows, as well as the Half-Bridge Scow, were all operated by Hank Wickman from 1914 till the end of the fishwheel era, under lease from Seufert Brothers. The Half-Bridge dipper was located near the old Highway 30 overhead-crossing, at the entrance to The Dalles-Celilo Canal, and was so-called because, at this point, the railroad track was laid with one rail on the ground and the other supported by a timber bridge.

Among the many scows in the vicinity of The Dalles, Oscar Charley had two portable wheels which he fished above Sturgeon Lake, on the north side of the river east of the city. He also operated one on the north bank opposite Seufert Wheel No. 5, approximately at the site of the old Washington Wheel, which was destroyed by the 1894 flood.

Oscar Charley was a large, erect, fine-looking Indian (a baseball pitcher in his youth) who dressed well and wore a tie when he went into town. He apparently profited from his fishing enterprise because he bought a new car each year for many years, first being partial to Overlands and then Buicks. He would remove the rear-seat cushions and haul wet fish in these fine cars, trading for a new car rather than cleaning out the old automobile at the end of the season.

During an interview, Kennedy Cathlamet, Oscar Charley's son, related how he performed the disagreeable task of oiling the babbited axle bearings of his father's scow wheels by climbing out on the booms over dangerous water. "The oil would run out of those bearings as fast as you poured it in," was his comment. He also related how another of his father's units drifted downstream and broke up on Threemile Rapids. Oscar Charley died, May 1, 1955.

Other Indians who operated or managed floating wheels at various periods in this area were Jake Andrews, Ole Charley, Mary Charley, Ida Thomas, Henry Thomas, Joe St. Martin, and Elva Charley.

Upstream, C. M. Stone operated a floating wheel in 1896, fishing it alongside the crib of the old Klickitat No. 1 stationary dipper, which washed out in the 1894 flood. In 1897, Caleb Hill had a scow unit on Rabbit (Brown's) Island at a point nearly opposite the China Pete stationary fishwheels. Hill and Reese later fished the scow in partnership.

Other wheels in the area included the Frank Wheel and two Klickitat wheels—and there are bits of evidence to indicate that additional fishing machines may have been built by those who "got the fever." It is certain that many of these attempts, while starting with confidence, ended in complete failure. Among them was the Creston Brown Wheel on Rabbit Island. According to information available, this wheel had no outside crib or wall to keep fish penned in the dipway. It was mere luck if fish entered one of its dips. Brown called it a "basket" wheel.

Hans Blaser, of The Dalles, recalled the Haskens Scow, which he said was built about 1906 and located a mile or so below The Dalles Bridge on the Oregon shore. It ran for three or four years but proved unsuccessful and was permitted to go to "wrack and ruin." There are some old-timers, however, who believe this machine was really one of Sam Williams' scows.

Indians gaffing salmon at Celilo Falls. Two of the three Taffe wheels, in bad repair, are visible in background. (Oregon Historical Society)

West of Seufert's Cannery, scows are stored in eddy just above Threemile Rapids. Shaker Church can be seen on point. (Edra Ann Dielschneider)

INDIAN SHAKER CHURCH

One of the interesting historical vignettes of The Dalles area concerns Sam Williams, a well-educated Indian who became wealthy, according to the standards of that day, by operating scow wheels in the vicinity of Big Eddy. His pioneer parents, en route to Sturgeon Lake, were crossing the frozen Columbia when they broke through the ice and were drowned. Young Sam, no more than four years old at the time, was then cared for at the Catholic Mission Academy for several years. Later he was sent to the Chemawa Indian School, near Salem, in the Willamette Valley. During these later years he developed a deep sense of religion, and upon returning to The Dalles, established a small Indian Shaker Church where he preached his own brand of philosophy.

This weathered little church still stands on the lava basalt overlooking the Columbia, about 200 feet east of The Dalles Bridge. The building might hold 20 people comfortably. However, when Hans Blaser and his brother attended Williams' church services, only three or four Indian worshipers were present. The minister had an old straight-horn Victrola phonograph on which he played a recording of an odd musical chant.

Several chairs and a bench or two were provided for worshipers, but older Indians preferred to sit on their blankets placed upon the ground. Above the door was nailed a sign, now almost obliterated by decades of sun, wind, and rain, which reads: "Indian Shaker Church—You are welcome—Please be orderly—No rowdyism allowed—Minister, Sam Williams." This sign is on exhibit at the Winquatt Museum.

CHINA PETE WHEELS

In the 1890s, The Dalles Packing and Canning Company, located at the foot of Laughlin Street, built the Upper and Lower China Pete salmon wheels near Eightmile Rapids, at Dillon along the Oregon shore, on land homesteaded by the company owners, Everding and Farrell. These Portland merchants had earlier established the Pillar Rock Packing Company.

When the company decided to construct the wheels, they persuaded Ah Fook to move there and help build them, as he was adept with hammer and saw. Ah Fook, a Chinese truck gardener at The Dalles in the early days, was, as it happened, addicted to gambling in his spare time. How long he worked there is not known, but as attested to by one old-timer, his spare-time addiction to gambling brought results that occasioned his sudden departure on a midnight freight for friendlier climes. Someone hung the "monicker" "China Pete" on Ah Fook, and the wheels picked up the name.

The Upper China Pete Wheel was more successful than the Lower because it was set in swifter water and revolved faster. Following gradual deterioration, the Upper China Pete dipper was rebuilt in 1922 with concrete cribbing. This modified design was made by a professional engineer who had worked on The Dalles-Celilo Canal, the only wheel design in the area supervised by one with such training. Catch records of the Upper and Lower China Pete Wheels were combined in company records and were simply called "China Pete." The highest yearly catch by these dippers was made in 1906, when 48,610 pounds of salmon were taken. The average catch over their lifetime was about 11 tons per year.

A story is told of how, about 1925, someone started the Upper China Pete Wheel fishing during the week-end closure period. A serious fine could be levied against any operator for violating the weekend "curfew" or cessation of wheel operation. For this reason most tenders were careful to comply. At the peak of the various fish runs, operators were in almost constant daylight attendance at their wheels, but in their absence, poachers would sneak into the structure, break the securing chains or locks, lower the wheel, and fish for a time, departing with the salmon they wanted and sometimes not even bothering to stop the wheel when they had finished. This is what they say happened at the China Pete Wheel:

During a week-end closure, someone had set the wheel fishing and an officer reported this to the company, but Chris Peterson and Clarence Fargher had already discovered the violation as they were en route to Celilo. When they crossed over to stop the wheel, they found 900 pounds of fish in the receiving box. Since the fish had been taken during a closed period, they belonged to the State of Oregon.

Cyclone Wheel in reconstructed form. Fish caught by this wheel, and by Bay and Little wheels downstream, were transported in cable car over the water to the fishery on the Oregon shore for transport to Seufert's Cannery by wagon, railroad car, or motor truck, depending upon the era. (University of Oregon Library)

Looking downstream toward Big Eddy, The Dalles, and Mt. Hood. Bay Wheel, formerly Cove Wheel, shows at right on Washington shore. Built by The Dalles Packing Company in the 1890s, it was rebuilt at least three times—with a stone and mortar cribbing or base, with a wooden rock-filled cribbing as pictured here, and with a final concrete cribbing. (Oregon Historical Society)

ON THE WASHINGTON SIDE

The China Pete Wheels continued to be a landmark until 1948, when they were destroyed by the flood waters of that year. In addition to these wheels, The Dalles Packing Company built several other stationary wheels during the 1890s, including the Bluejay, the Bay, the Little, and the Cyclone, all on its Washington lands, and all of which properties were later sold to Seufert Brothers.

The Bluejay Stationary was situated on the rocky river bank directly across from the cannery at a site now enclosed by the powerhouse at The Dalles Dam. Seuferts abandoned the Bluejay soon after purchase, and scow wheels later fished at the site. One of the main reasons for its abandonment was the inability of the company's steam-powered launch to reach the wheel during high water for transporting catches to the cannery. A few years after the Bluejay was abandoned, however, the wooden-hulled, gasoline-operated salmon tender, *Lillie*, was built and traversed all these waters.

Between Big Eddy and the head of Fivemile Rapids the Columbia contained some of the swiftest and most violent waters in its entire course. Veteran

wheel tender, Chris Kitto, believed salmon entered the eddy one day and left the next. At dawn he would observe the salmon leaving the eddy. By 9:00 a.m. the Bay Wheel, less than 200 yards upstream, would be reaching its peak catch of the day, followed by a peak at the Cyclone Wheel, 300 yards or so farther upstream, 3 to 6 hours later. The Cyclone's best record was in 1913 when it caught 225,165 pounds of salmon. Its average catch was 22 tons per season.

Prior to 1907, it took all day for a horse-drawn wagon with a load (about 1½ tons) of salmon to make the round trip between the Cyclone Wheel and The Dalles Packing Company, by way of The Dalles Ferry. Upon assuming ownership, Seuferts installed a cableway across the Columbia River from the Cyclone Wheel to the Fishery, near No. 4 dipper, to transport fish caught by all three of these wheels to the Oregon shore, there to be hauled by wagon, and later by truck, to the cannery. . . . The Cyclone was burned to the ground by workmen at The Dalles Dam Project on October 26, 1956.

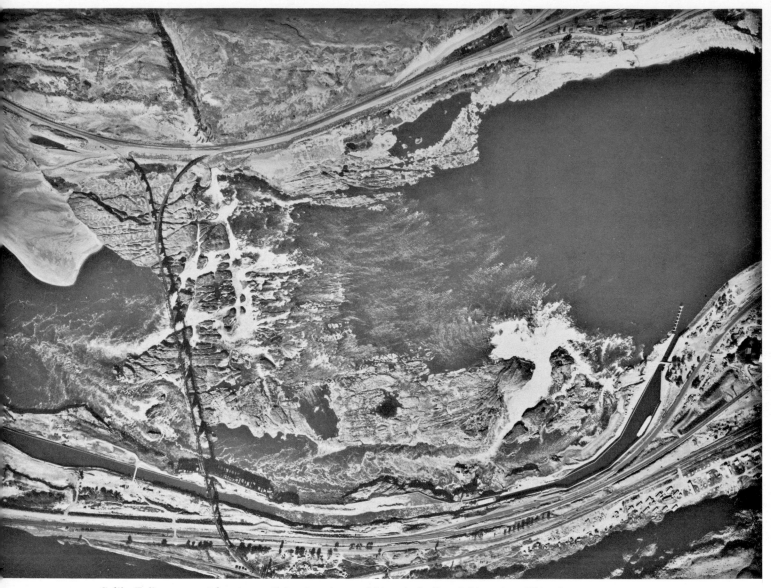

Celilo Falls—natural barrier to fish migration and historic Indian fishing site. This view was taken October 10, 1956, prior to inundation by The Dalles Dam. (U. S. Corps of Engineers)

View showing Taffe operation at Celilo, including fishwheels and cannery before construction of The Dalles-Celilo Canal. The wheels were built by Taffe in the early 1890s. Indian camp is in foreground. (Oregon Historical Society)

AT CELILO

Upriver in the Celilo area, I. H. Taffe was a large-scale and successful wheel man, with three wheels and a fish cannery built in the late 1880s. The cannery had a capacity of some 10 tons a day. Taffe had been a "Johnny Reb" in the Confederate Army and was a "bearcat" with a short-fused temper. More than one Indian got buckshot in his back for trying to fish in the small basalt channel leading to one of his dippers.

Centuries before the arrival of the "Boston men," Indian dipnetters and spearmen had learned that salmon follow water-filled natural channels in the lava. White men, when they came, also noted this and turned it to their advantage. Taffe reasoned that fish would enter a man-made waterway as well as one provided by nature. About 1886, he excavated a wide, deep ditch in hard lava on property he owned at the upper rim of Celilo Falls. When the broken basalt was removed following the blasting operation, the channel served as an effective avenue of approach to one of his three wheels. Water rushed with alarming swiftness and turbulence down this sluiceway, while the fish surged up it in numbers astounding to modern fishway designers. In The Dalles-Celilo region several of the most successful wheel sites had similar "cuts" blasted out of the lava as approach-ways to wheel dippers.

Two of the Taffe wheels were located at the head of Celilo Falls on the Oregon shore. In 1899, a very long, horizontal-bar fish lead was constructed, extending westerly from these wheels toward Chief's Island. This lead did not effectively divert salmon to the dippers, and when ice destroyed the lead a year later, it was not rebuilt. Much more productive was a third wheel that Taffe built near the head of The Dalles-Celilo Canal, in the small channel he had constructed there.

All the Taffe salmon wheels were low-water dippers built primarily for fall fishing, but they could catch spring fish if the river flow was relatively low. This was in contrast to most of the other fishwheels in The Dalles-Celilo area, which were designed to turn in the spring during the higher-flow periods. If the Columbia remained relatively high in June and for part of July, the latter wheels could continue to operate, but in the fall, the river was too low, permitting only the fall-run wheels to turn.

After 1927, Indian dipnetters took over the rocky channel blasted by Taffe at Celilo Falls, which had delivered tons of fish annually to his wheel. At least one small adventuresome Indian owed his life to the dipnetters near the bottom end of Taffe's channel. Native fishermen used dipnets there to take fish ascending the wild raceway. About 1948 an Indian fisherman felt a large object enter his net. He quickly pulled in the net to claim his bounty, but to his surprise, there emerged a very wet, gasping Indian boy who had fallen from the precipitous walls above.

Indians dipnetting in Downes' Channel at Celilo, which led to the best of the three wheels that Taffe built in the early 1890s. The wheel superstructure shows at upper left of photo, which was taken after fishwheels were banned in Oregon. The channel indicates the velocities that salmon swam through in large numbers. (U. S. Corps of Engineers)

Two of the three Taffe wheels at Celilo during low water, prior to construction of The Dalles-Celilo Canal. Two fishleads can be seen below the wheels. (Oregon Historical Society)

END OF AN ERA

In any discussion of fishwheels, inevitably the questions arise—How many fish did the wheels catch? Were they truly murderous machines? Did each catch fish by the hundreds of thousands, as was stated by some and believed by many? Were fishwheels a significant factor in the decline of the salmon runs in the Columbia River? . . . Factual information is available and will help answer these questions.

During the period from 1879 to 1935, there were at least 79 different stationary wheels on the Columbia. Perhaps seven of these can be considered truly outstanding because they caught fish adequately every year, were dependable, and either set or nearly achieved record catches. These were the real bread-and-butter machines. In The Dalles-Celilo area, five stationary wheels were in this category: No. 5, Tumwater No. 1, Cement, Tumwater No. 2, and Cyclone.

In the Cascades region, Warren Packing Company's Wheels 16 and B-1 seemed to be the best. It is possible that other dippers were as good or even better, but either official records do not exist or could not be found to prove this. Available catch records indicate that Seuferts' No. 5 was the best wheel on the Columbia River and probably in the world. This wheel caught 4,625,776 pounds of salmon in 31 years of operation, averaging 149,218 pounds per season, or about 75 tons.

To the surprise of no one acquainted with various fishwheels in the United States and elsewhere, the presence of the efficient and picturesque fishwheels (or infernal engines of destruction, depending upon who was talking) led to almost endless "fish fights" in the Oregon Legislature. In the move to outlaw these wheels, the statements of each side were strongly biased toward their own position. On one side were the "Cascade Locks-The Dalles-Celilo Operators"; on the other, the lower river "Astoria Bunch."

While both sides in these verbal battles argued that conservation was a good thing, and that it was necessary to perpetuate the salmon runs for future use, both sides were likewise convinced that if the "greedy adversary" (the "opposition") would only take less fish—or if their gear were outlawed—then the salmon runs would be saved. The battle was long and heated with considerable "horse-trading" politics thrown in. An interesting account of one of the many battles in these "fish fights" appeared in the *Oregonian*, February 11, 1923, as follows:

"When Lower Columbia River wasn't swatting Upper Columbia, it was because Upper Columbia was swatting back in course of an alleged 'harmony' meeting of the house committee on fisheries, called to hear arguments and adjust differences in proposed fishing legislation last night. The only harmony at the meeting was the unanimity of purpose with which the two salmon fishing factions flew at each other's throats. Most of the session was taken up with charges and counter charges, exciting personal altercations and words between witnesses and each other and members of the committee.

"Lower river charged that Upper river fishermen are putting the salmon industry out of business, and Upper river interests related that 95 salmon are caught and canned on the Lower Columbia to every five fish on the Upper river. This brought from the Lower river men the specific charge that Upper river seines in the employ of Seufert kill millions of unborn salmon by trampling spawn on the seining grounds.

"One interesting development was the declaration by F. M. Warren, Jr., an Upper river cannery operator, that irrigating ditches along the Upper river are the greatest menace the salmon fishery industry has. This was seconded by Seufert, who said that irrigation has caused the extermination of the famous blueback salmon. This fish, he said, spawns in natural lakes, and its young must mature in the calm lake waters before braving the turbulent river currents, or they do not survive. He declared that following irrigation development of such lakes as Wallowa Lake, hundreds of young salmon have died in the irrigation ditches and that the blueback salmon has been exterminated. This explanation of the extermination of the bluebacks was challenged by Representative Belland, a member of the Committee. . . ."

Perhaps the most important factor in these battles between the groups, although it was scarcely mentioned openly and lurked beneath the surface, was Seufert Brothers Company's low-cost raw material, obtained by their wheels and Celilo seines, as compared to the cost of the fish to the Lower river operators.

The *Oregon Voter* pamphlet, issued prior to the General Election of Tuesday, November 2, 1926, contained spirited arguments on each side concerning the fishwheel, trap, and drag seine bill contained in the official ballot. The affirmative argument (to eliminate these types of gear) was subscribed to by the Oregon State Grange, Oregon State Federation of Labor, and the Fish Commission of Oregon. The negative argument, in opposition to eliminating such gear, was subscribed to by The Dalles-Wasco Chamber of Commerce. In essence, the affirmative argument, while admitting that fishwheels took only a small percentage of the catch, maintained that all fish escaping tidewater should be allowed to proceed on upstream, that two families (Seufert and Warren) took 85 per cent of the fish caught above tidewater and employed relatively few men in their operations, and that a few fishwheels took as many fish in 24 hours as the average gill-net fisherman took in 4 years of labor.

The negative argument—which incidentally had the support of Astoria newspapers—also maintained that the bill was initiated by a group of vote-seeking politicians, and that the purpose of the bill was to monopolize the fishing industry and thereby control the price of fish to the consuming public. They quoted Henry O'Malley, then U. S. Commissioner of Fisheries, in his May 18, 1926, letter to Hugh C. Mitchell of Portland, as saying: "Each form of gear used is responsible for depletion in proportion to the number of fish it takes," and he advised there was no need for more regulation. The negative position closed their argument with asking by what American principle of fair dealing could the takers of 88 per cent of the fish demand confiscation of the large investments in equipment, factories, and labor of those who took less than 7 per cent of the fish.

Sign that Frank A. Seufert painted in 1927 on horse-barn roof at the cannery after fishwheels were declared illegal in Oregon. The sign was removed in 1929. (Oregon Historical Society)

View of Seufert Brothers Company Salmon and Fruit Cannery about 1928. Wooden cattle bridge crosses Fifteenmile Creek between Highway U. S. 30 Bridge, left, and Union Pacific Railroad Bridge. Mt. Hood and City of The Dalles are in background. (Oregon Historical Society)

After the vote of November 2, 1926, was counted, it was found that the years of controversy, legislative battles, court decrees, and involvement by many groups were over, and that the people of Oregon outlawed, from that time on, the use of fishwheels in the state. In November 1934, the people of the State of Washington followed the earlier Oregon example by outlawing further use of these dippers. Thus ended the fishwheel era on the Columbia River.

Seuferts' No. 5 fishwheel and its ready accessibility to the Columbia River Highway may have been the immediate cause of outlawing all wheels on the river. This was certainly the most productive dipper on the Upper river, probably better than any other ever built on the Columbia, and was the one always referred to in the endless "fish fights." It reared its powerful structure on the south shore, a few paces from Route 30, where Astoria fishermen, with their hatred of all wheels and traps, would stop and replenish their spleen by viewing fish taken so "effortlessly."

In their wrath, and enlisting the aid of the Oregon State Grange, the Astorians spread damaging reports of wasted fish and destruction of the runs. Thus, in 1926, after 42 years of effort, they made law of Judge Matthew P. Deady's condemnation of

March 26, 1884, when he wrote: ". . . But I cannot refrain from adding, on behalf of the public, that I think the best disposition which could be made of this controversy would be for the Legislature to intervene in the interest of the fish of the future and prohibit these murderous machines anywhere in the waters of the state."

The long-drawn-out "fishwheel fight" on the Columbia was actually not fought for conservation, as depicted. Rather, the compelling reasons were economic, each side striving to catch as many fish as possible, with the low-cost production on the Upper river being particularly irritating to the Lower-river operators. Closure of the fishwheels probably made little difference in catches at the wheel sites, at least in The Dalles-Celilo area. Gill nets set in eddies below dipway entrances and dip-netters in the wheel channels continued to take salmon that otherwise would have been captured by the revolving fishing machines.

Now, aside from a few pilings and rocks and a model or two, only the story of the fishwheels and fading memories are left as reminders of the time—not too many years ago—when fish were lifted from the waters of the Columbia by the dippers of many turning wheels along this great stream.

113

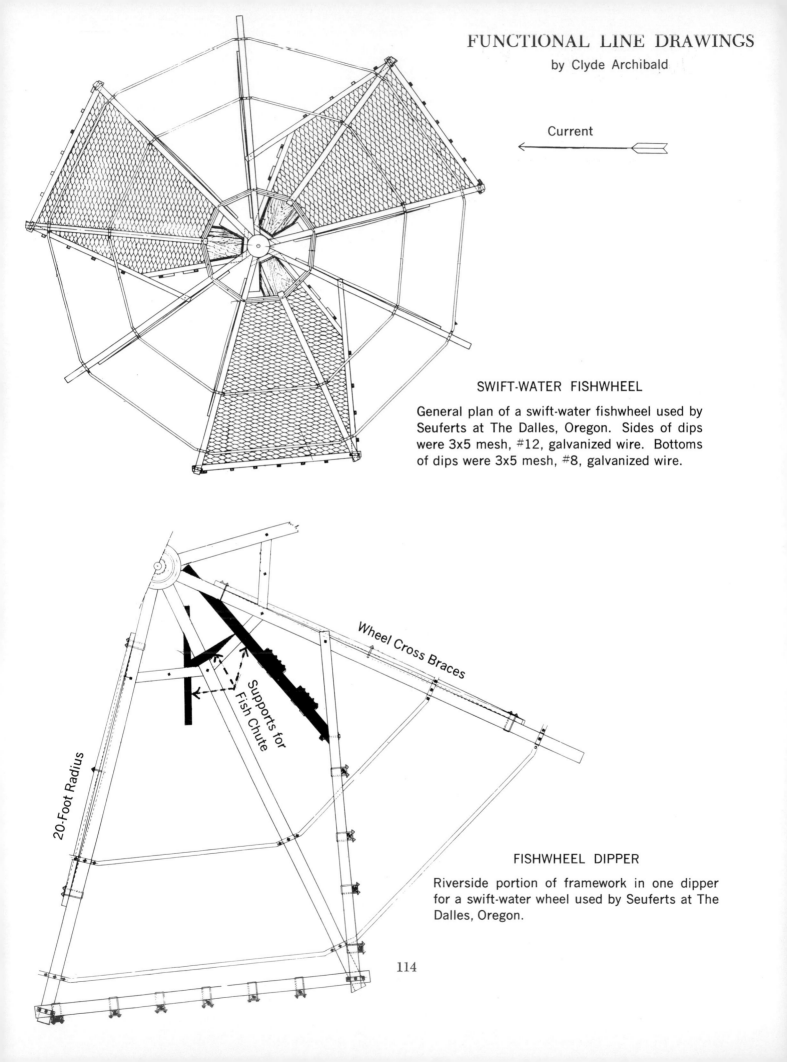

FUNCTIONAL LINE DRAWINGS
by Clyde Archibald

Current

SWIFT-WATER FISHWHEEL

General plan of a swift-water fishwheel used by Seuferts at The Dalles, Oregon. Sides of dips were 3x5 mesh, #12, galvanized wire. Bottoms of dips were 3x5 mesh, #8, galvanized wire.

Wheel Cross Braces

Supports for Fish Chute

20-Foot Radius

FISHWHEEL DIPPER

Riverside portion of framework in one dipper for a swift-water wheel used by Seuferts at The Dalles, Oregon.

114

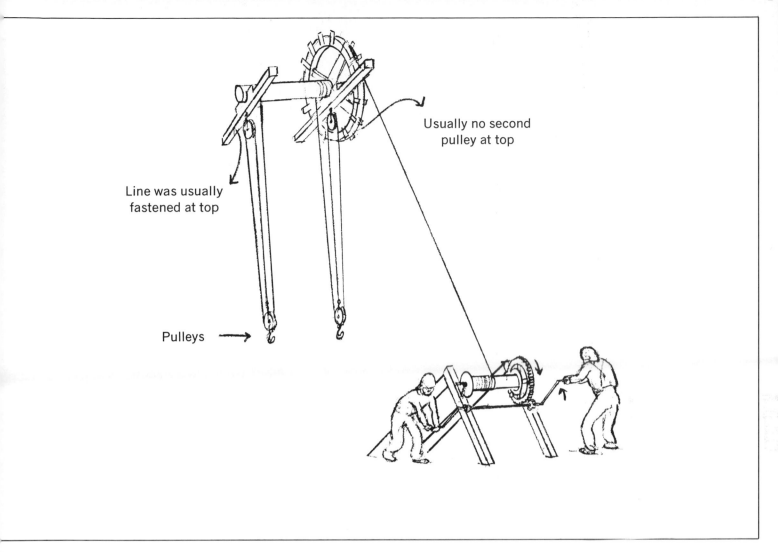

Usually no second
pulley at top

Line was usually
fastened at top

Pulleys →

THE BULLWHEEL

Diagram of system used for lifting the assembly of a fishwheel. The bullwheel was the main driving gear, with pulleys being attached to the rotating assembly of the wheel to raise or lower it—and to remove it from the water during off seasons. See page 25.

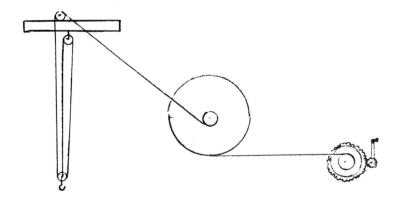

Side view of lifting apparatus showing relationship of line on pulleys, bullwheel, and gear wheel.

115

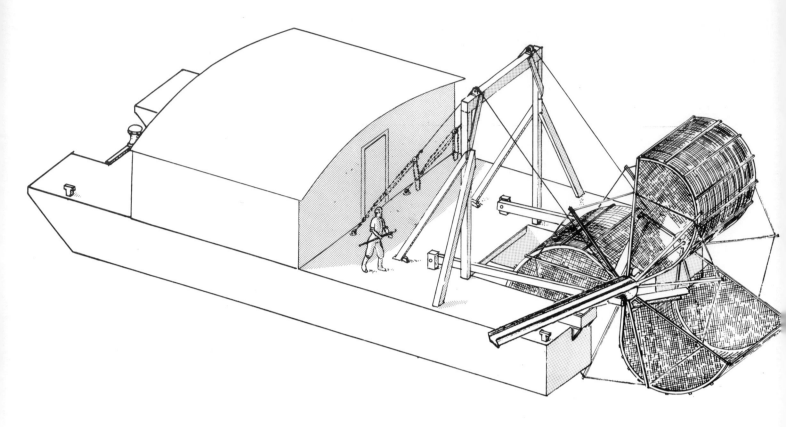

SCOW FISHWHEEL

Transition-type catamaran scow fishwheel. The two lumber floats and twin booms with rotor mounted thereon—plus rotor elevation or lowering mechanism—were definite advances over the log-float type of catamaran. The fish chute discharged into the receiving scow tied alongside. Dippers were slanted toward scow for rapid discharge. Winch for operating the pulleys was housed in the cabin, which was living quarters for the crew. The capstan (far left) was used to winch the structure upstream. The cleat by the chute was used for securing the line to the receiving scow. See page 49.

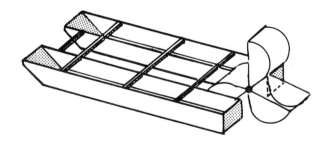

OPEN-BILGE SCOW

Basic structure of open-bilge type of scow, which received the fish directly into the bilge.

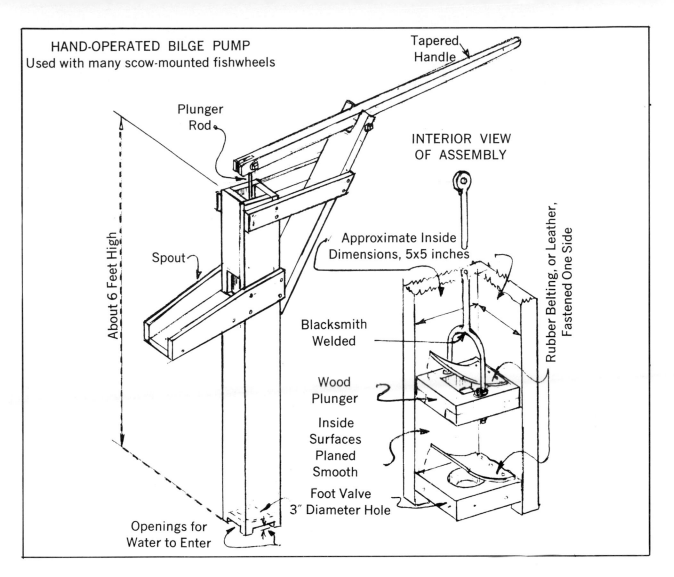

HAND-OPERATED BILGE PUMP
Used with many scow-mounted fishwheels

Tapered Handle

Plunger Rod

INTERIOR VIEW OF ASSEMBLY

About 6 Feet High

Spout

Approximate Inside Dimensions, 5x5 inches

Rubber Belting, or Leather, Fastened One Side

Blacksmith Welded

Wood Plunger

Inside Surfaces Planed Smooth

Foot Valve 3″ Diameter Hole

Openings for Water to Enter

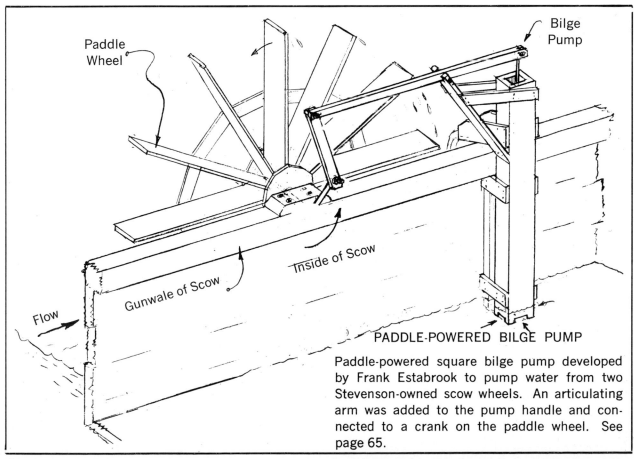

Paddle Wheel

Bilge Pump

Flow

Gunwale of Scow

Inside of Scow

PADDLE-POWERED BILGE PUMP

Paddle-powered square bilge pump developed by Frank Estabrook to pump water from two Stevenson-owned scow wheels. An articulating arm was added to the pump handle and connected to a crank on the paddle wheel. See page 65.

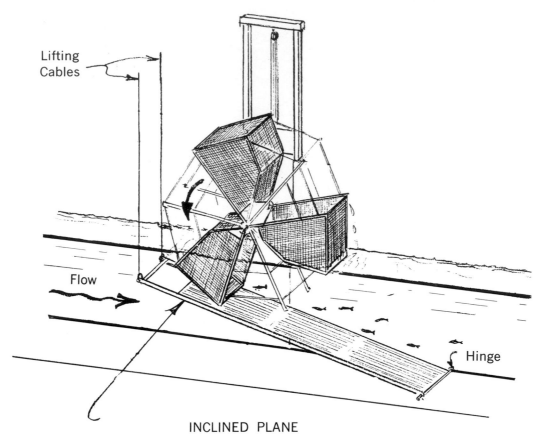

Lifting
Cables

Flow

Hinge

INCLINED PLANE

Cutaway of fish lead to show use of inclined
plane to guide fish up to wheel. Plane was
made of slatted lumber.

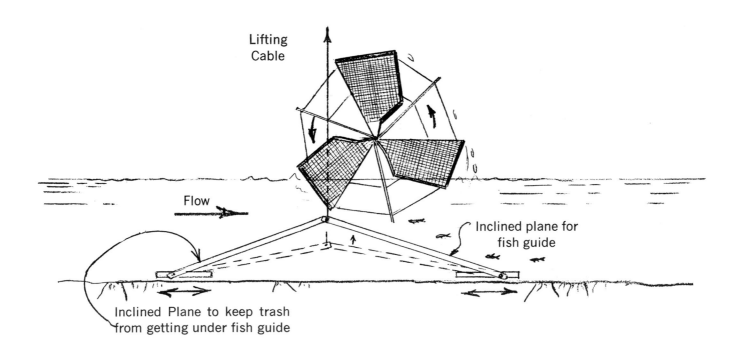

Lifting
Cable

Flow

Inclined plane for
fish guide

Inclined Plane to keep trash
from getting under fish guide

118

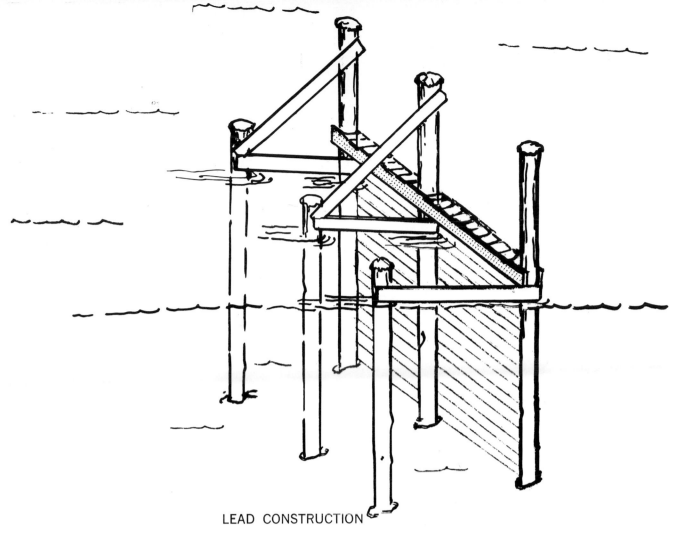

LEAD CONSTRUCTION

Plan view of horizontal-bar lead and brace piling, showing work platform above water surface on the lead or upstream row of piling. Note the triangular braces. Some wheel men pulled the tops of the two rows of piling together, and lashed them in that position. See pages 58 and 59.

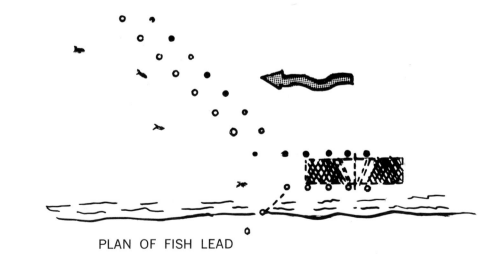

PLAN OF FISH LEAD

Plan view of a fishwheel rotor on the right and a long row of lead and brace piling angling downstream from the dipway.

RIVER CHARTS OF FISHWHEELS

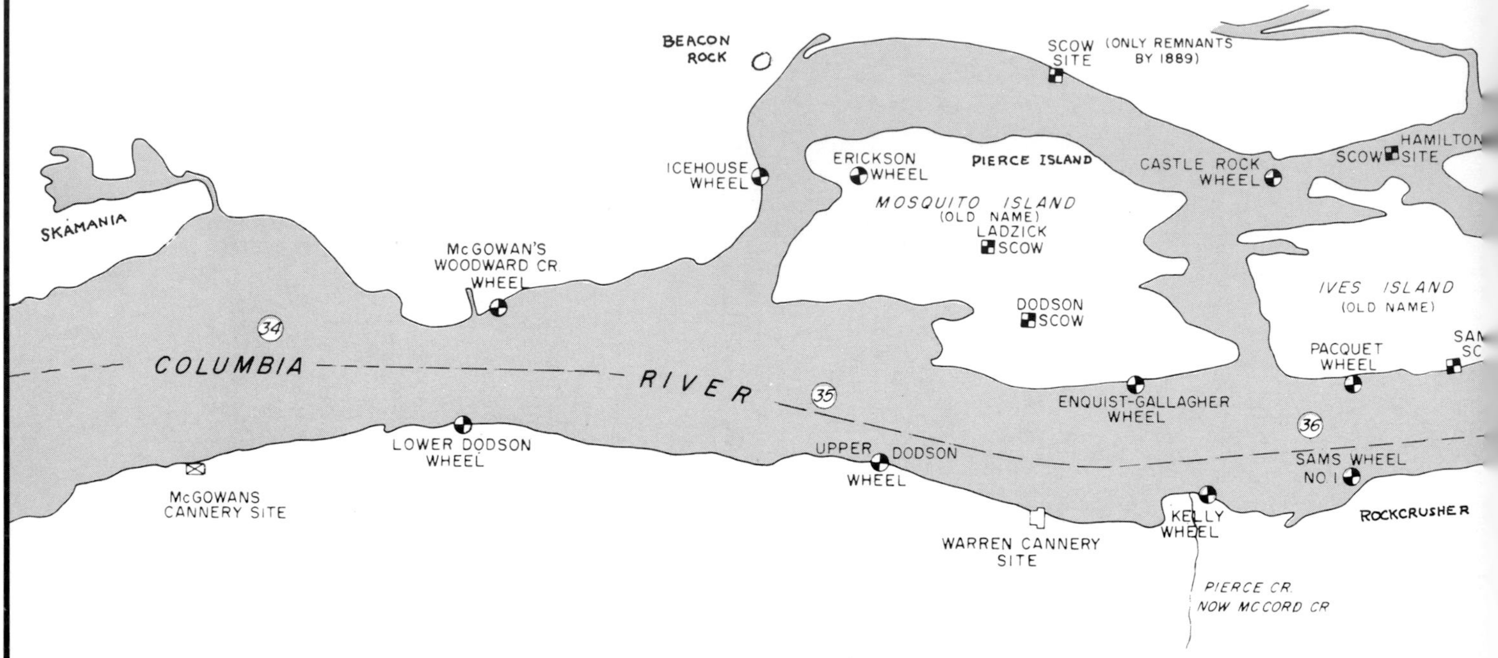

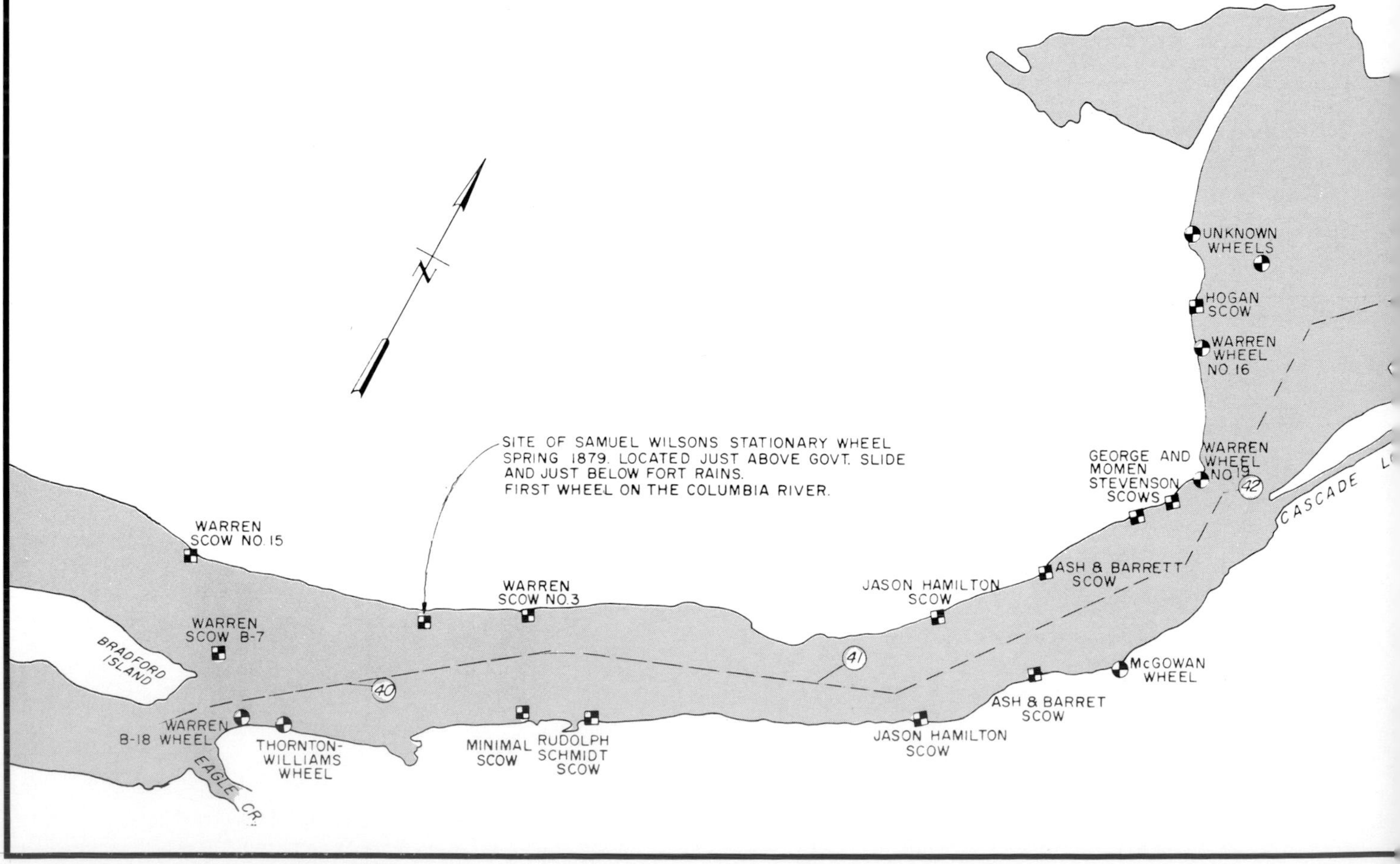

BEACON ROCK

SCOW SITE (ONLY REMNANTS BY 1889)

ICEHOUSE WHEEL

ERICKSON WHEEL

PIERCE ISLAND

CASTLE ROCK WHEEL

SCOW SITE

HAMILTON

MOSQUITO ISLAND (OLD NAME)

McGOWAN'S WOODWARD CR. WHEEL

LADZICK SCOW

IVES ISLAND (OLD NAME)

SKAMANIA

34

COLUMBIA

DODSON SCOW

RIVER

35

ENQUIST-GALLAGHER WHEEL

PACQUET WHEEL

SAMS SC

LOWER DODSON WHEEL

UPPER DODSON WHEEL

36

SAMS WHEEL NO.1

McGOWANS CANNERY SITE

WARREN CANNERY SITE

KELLY WHEEL

ROCKCRUSHER

PIERCE CR. NOW MCCORD CR

UNKNOWN WHEELS

HOGAN SCOW

WARREN WHEEL NO.16

SITE OF SAMUEL WILSONS STATIONARY WHEEL
SPRING 1879. LOCATED JUST ABOVE GOVT. SLIDE
AND JUST BELOW FORT RAINS.
FIRST WHEEL ON THE COLUMBIA RIVER.

GEORGE AND MOMEN STEVENSON SCOWS

WARREN WHEEL NO.19

42

CASCADE LO

WARREN SCOW NO.15

WARREN SCOW NO.3

JASON HAMILTON SCOW

ASH & BARRETT SCOW

WARREN SCOW B-7

BRADFORD ISLAND

41

McGOWAN WHEEL

40

ASH & BARRET SCOW

WARREN B-18 WHEEL

THORNTON-WILLIAMS WHEEL

MINIMAL SCOW

RUDOLPH SCHMIDT SCOW

JASON HAMILTON SCOW

EAGLE CR.

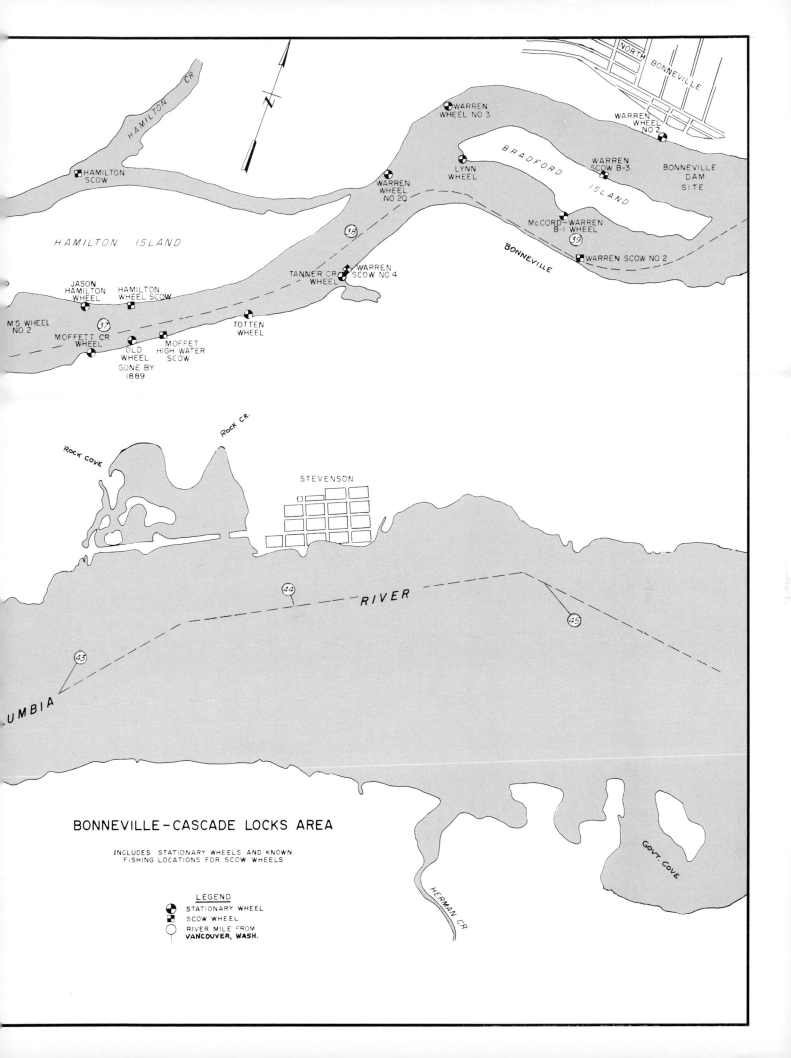

BONNEVILLE-CASCADE LOCKS AREA

INCLUDES STATIONARY WHEELS AND KNOWN
FISHING LOCATIONS FOR SCOW WHEELS

LEGEND
STATIONARY WHEEL
SCOW WHEEL
RIVER MILE FROM
VANCOUVER, WASH.

RIVER CHARTS OF FISHWHEELS

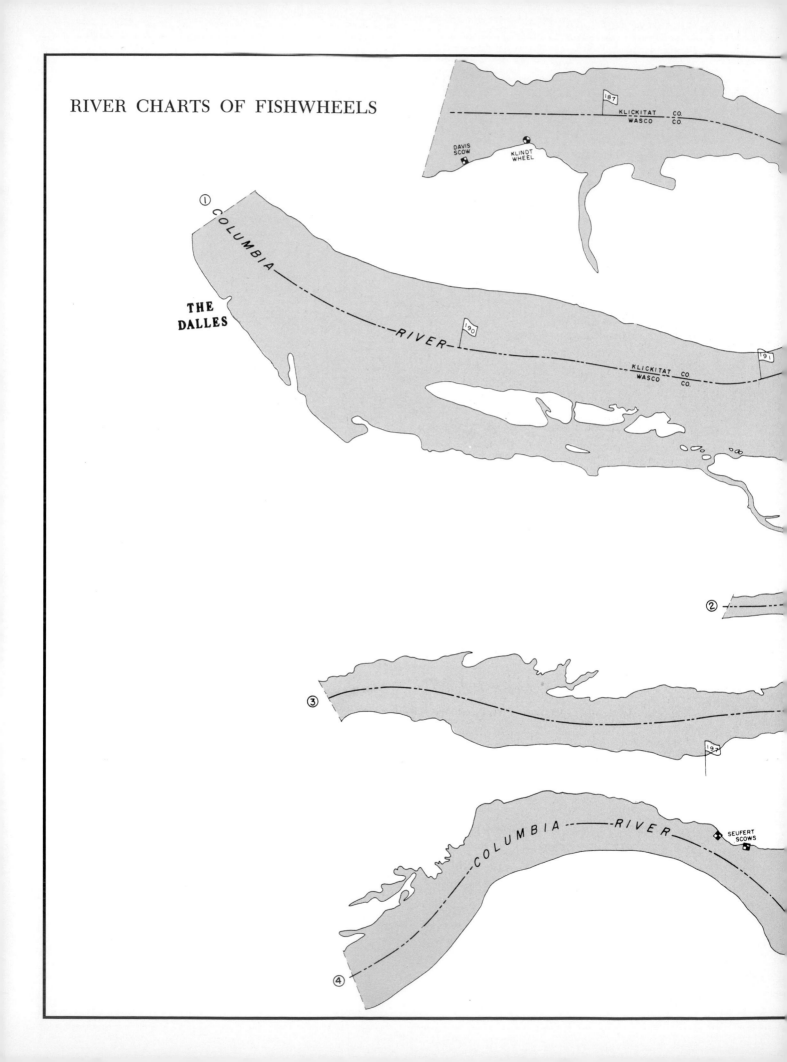

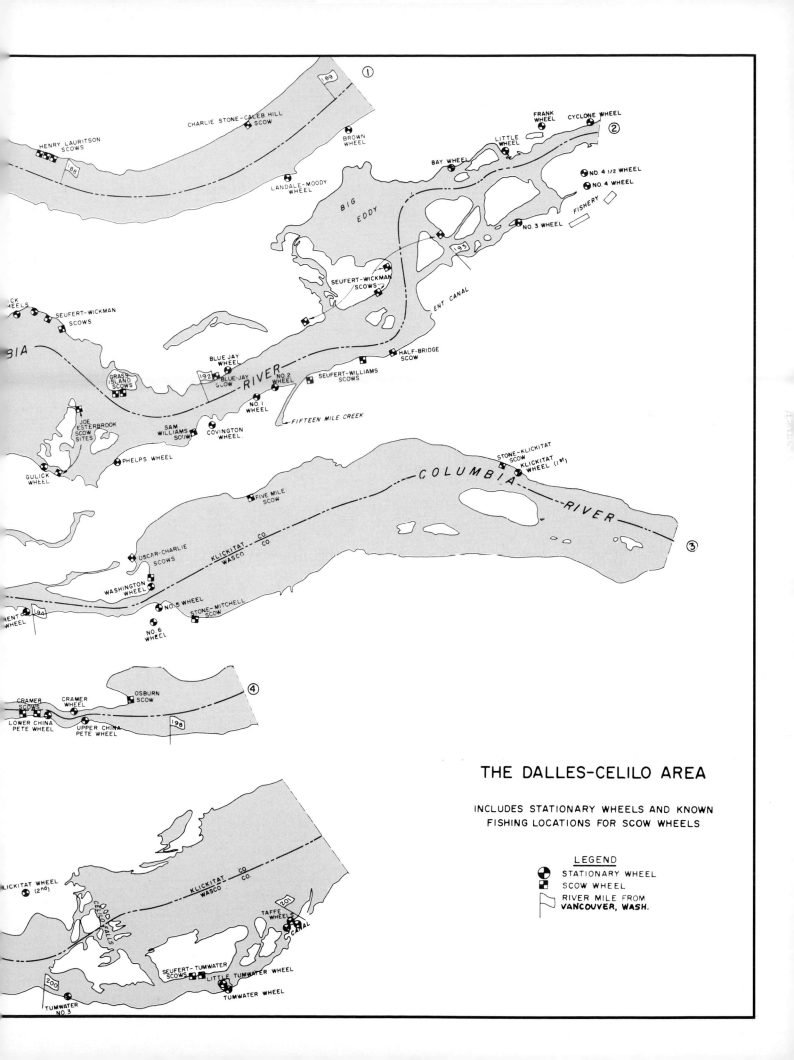

THE DALLES-CELILO AREA

INCLUDES STATIONARY WHEELS AND KNOWN
FISHING LOCATIONS FOR SCOW WHEELS

LEGEND
STATIONARY WHEEL
SCOW WHEEL
RIVER MILE FROM
VANCOUVER, WASH.

CHARLIE STONE-CALEB HILL SCOW
HENRY LAURITSON SCOWS
BROWN WHEEL
LANDALE-MOODY WHEEL
BIG EDDY
FRANK WHEEL
CYCLONE WHEEL
LITTLE WHEEL
BAY WHEEL
NO. 4 1/2 WHEEL
NO. 4 WHEEL
FISHERY
NO. 3 WHEEL
ENT CANAL
SEUFERT-WICKMAN SCOWS
CK EELS
SEUFERT-WICKMAN SCOWS
BIA
GRASS ISLAND SCOWS
JOE ESTERBROOK SCOW SITES
GULICK WHEEL
PHELPS WHEEL
SAM WILLIAMS SCOW
COVINGTON WHEEL
BLUE JAY WHEEL
BLUE JAY SCOW
NO. 2 WHEEL
NO. 1 WHEEL
SEUFERT-WILLIAMS SCOWS
HALF-BRIDGE SCOW
RIVER
FIFTEEN MILE CREEK
COLUMBIA
RIVER
STONE-KLICKITAT SCOW
KLICKITAT WHEEL (1st)
FIVE MILE SCOW
OSCAR-CHARLIE SCOWS
KLICKITAT CO. CO.
WASCO
WASHINGTON WHEEL
NO. 5 WHEEL
STONE-MITCHELL SCOW
NO. 6 WHEEL
ENT WHEEL
CRAMER SCOWS
CRAMER WHEEL
OSBURN SCOW
LOWER CHINA PETE WHEEL
UPPER CHINA PETE WHEEL
KLICKITAT WHEEL (2nd)
KLICKITAT CO. CO.
WASCO
TAFFE WHEELS
CANAL
CELILO FALLS
SEUFERT-TUMWATER SCOWS
LITTLE TUMWATER WHEEL
TUMWATER WHEEL
TUMWATER NO. 3

189
188
195
192
194
198
200
201

BIBLIOGRAPHY

BEAN, TARLETON H. (1894) Bibliography of the salmon of Alaska and adjacent regions. U.S. Fish Commission, Fishery Bulletin, vol. 12, for 1892, pp.39-49.

BROGAN, PHIL F. (1971) East of the Cascades. Binfords & Mort, Portland, Oregon, 304 pp.

BROWN, DONALD A. (1935) History of the Cascades. MS., 81 pp.

CAREY, CHARLES H. (1971) General history of Oregon. Binfords & Mort, Portland, Oregon, 968 pp.

COBB, JOHN N. (1911) The salmon fisheries of the Pacific Coast. U.S. Bureau of Fisheries, Report of the Commissioner of Fisheries for the fiscal year 1910 and special papers (Document 751), 179 pp.

COBB, JOHN N. (1917) Pacific salmon fisheries. U.S. Bureau of Fisheries, Report of the Commissioner of Fisheries for the fiscal year 1916, Appendix III (Document 839), 255 pp.

COBB, JOHN N. (1922) Pacific salmon fisheries. 3rd ed. U.S. Bureau of Fisheries, Report of the Commissioner of Fisheries for the fiscal year 1921, Appendix I (Document 902), 268 pp.

CRAIG, JOSEPH A., and ROBERT L. HACKER. (1950) The history and development of the fisheries of the Columbia River. U.S. Bureau of Fisheries, Fishery Bulletin 32, pp. 133-216.

DEADY, MATTHEW PAUL. (1884) Judgment No. 826, William Rankin McCord vs. Samuel Wilson, rendered by Judge M. P. Deady in the U.S. District Court, Portland, Oregon.

DYRENFORTH, ROBERT G. (1887) Patents issued by the United States during the years 1882, 1883 and 1884, relating to fish and the methods, products and applications of the fisheries. U.S. Commission of Fish and Fisheries, Part 13, Report of the Commissioner for 1885, Appendix E, pp. 975-1099.

EVERETT, MARSHALL. (1912) Wreck and sinking of the Titanic, the ocean's greatest disaster. L. H. Walter, (no place of publication given), 320 pp.

GEORGE, M. C., Compiling author. (No date). The Columbia Highway through the Gorge of the Cascades from Portland to The Dalles. 40-50 pages.

HABERSHAM, ROBERT A. (1874) The Columbia River through the Cascade range, a map made under the direction of Major N. Michler. U.S. Corps of Engineers.

HEWES, GORDON WINANT. (1947) Aboriginal use of fishery resources in northwestern North America. University of California, 268 pp.

HOLDREDGE, CLAIRE P. (1937) Final geological report on the Bonneville Project. Oregon State Department of Geology and Mineral Industries, Portland, Oregon, 36 pp.

HOOD RIVER HISTORICAL SOCIETY. (195-) History of early pioneer families of Hood River, Oregon. Hood River, Oregon, 340 pp.

INGERSAL, ERNEST. (1883) A salmon wheel. Harpers Weekly, vol. 27, March 31, 1883, pp. 193, 198.

LAMPMAN, BEN HUR. (1946) The coming of the pond fishes; an account of the introduction of certain spiny-rayed fishes, and other exotic species, into the waters of the lower Columbia River region and the Pacific Coast states. Binfords & Mort, Portland, Oregon, 177 pp.

LANCASTER, SAMUEL CHRISTOPHER. (1915) Columbia, America's great highway through the Cascade Mountains to the sea. Author, Portland, Oregon, 140 pp.

LANCASTER, SAMUEL CHRISTOPHER. (1929) Romance of the gateway through the Cascade Range. The J. K. Gill Company, Portland, Oregon, 32 pp.

LOCKLEY, FRED. (1928) History of the Columbia River Valley from The Dalles to the sea. The S. J. Clarke Publishing Company, Chicago, vol. 1 (of 3 vols.)

LYMAN, WILLIAM DENISON. (1963) The Columbia River; its history, its myths, its scenery, its commerce. Binfords & Mort, Portland, Oregon, 416 pp.

McDONALD, MARSHALL. (1895) The salmon fisheries of the Columbia River basin. U.S. Fish Commission, Bulletin for 1894, vol. 14, pp. 153-168.

McNEAL, WILLIAM H. (195-) History of Wasco County, Oregon. The Dalles, Oregon, 471 pp.

MARSH, MILLARD C., and JOHN N. COBB. (1910) The fisheries of Alaska in 1908. U.S. Bureau of Fisheries, Report of the Commissioner of Fisheries for the fiscal year 1908 and special papers (Document 645), 78 pp.

MOFFETT, THOMAS; GEORGE STEVENSON, and others. (1860-1886) Road book for the County of Skamania, Washington Territory. MS.

NETBOY, ANTHONY. (1958) Salmon of the Pacific Northwest: fish vs. dams, Binfords & Mort, Portland, Oregon, 192 pp.

OREGON. STATE FISH COMMISSION. (1887-1956) Biennial reports. (Issuing office varies.)

RADCLIFFE, WILLIAM. (1921) Fishing from the earliest times. E. P. Dutton and Company, New York, 478 pp.

ROCKWELL, CLEVELAND. (1902) The great Columbia River basin. The Pacific Monthly, vol. 7, pp. 97-134.

ROSTLUND, ERHARD. (1952) Freshwater fish and fishing in native North America. University of California, Publications in Geography, No. 9, 313 pp.

SEUFERT, FRANCIS. (1955) Interview with Henry Wickman. MS.

SEUFERT, FRANCIS. Scrapbooks concerning fishing operations, The Dalles, Oregon.

SKAMANIA COUNTY AREA STUDY GROUP. HISTORY COMMITTEE. (1959) History of Skamania County. (mimeographed), Stevenson, Washington, 110 pp.

SMITH, HUGH M. (1895) Notes on a reconnaissance of the fisheries of the Pacific Coast of the United States in 1894. U.S. Fish Commission, Bulletin for 1894, vol. 14, pp. 223-288.

STONE, LIVINGSTON. (1897) The artificial propagation of salmon on the Pacific Coast of the United States, with notes on the natural history of the Quinnat salmon. U.S. Fish Commission, Bulletin for 1896, vol. 16, pp. 203-235.

STRONG, EMORY. (1967) Stone age on the Columbia River. Binfords & Mort, Portland, Oregon, 256 pp.

THWAITES, REUBEN GOLD, Editor. (1959) Original journals of the Lewis and Clark expedition, 1804-1806. Antiquarian Press, New York, 8 vols.

U. S. ARMY. CORPS OF ENGINEERS. (1938-64) Annual fish passage reports. North Pacific Division. Bonneville, The Dalles, McNary and Ice Harbor Dams, Columbia River, Oregon and Washington.

WILLIAMS, IRA A. (1923) The Columbia River gorge, its geologic history, interpreted from the Columbia River Highway. The Oregon Bureau of Mines and Geology, Portland, Oregon, 130 pp.

WILLIAMS, JOHN HARVEY. (1912) The guardians of the Columbia, Mount Hood, Mount Adams and Mount St. Helens. J. H. Williams, Tacoma, Washington, 144 pp.

WINANS, EPHRAIM. (1949-1950) Hood River as I have known it, as told to Doug Parker. Serialized in the Hood River News, Hood River, Oregon.

WRIGHT, E. W., Editor. (1895) Lewis & Dryden's marine history of the Pacific Northwest. The Lewis & Dryden Printing Company, Portland, Oregon, 518 pp.